WILLIAM HENRY BARTLETT

H. Room.

B. Holl.

W. H. BARTLETT.

Yours truly

W H Bartlett

William Henry Bartlett

Artist, Author, and Traveller

ALEXANDER M. ROSS

Containing a reprint of
Dr William Beattie's
Brief Memoir of the Late William Henry Bartlett

Mine is but the humble effort of a tourist,
to walk over the field which the learning and research of
others has rendered so fruitful,
and give a few impressions, and those
necessarily imperfect ones, of its actual
appearance to the eye.
THE NILE BOAT

UNIVERSITY OF TORONTO PRESS

© University of Toronto Press 1973
Toronto and Buffalo
Printed in Canada
ISBN 0-8020-1986-2
LC 72-97783

Contents

Preface

Theories of the picturesque and the sublime are at least as old as Joseph Addison, who noted how the imagination 'loves to be filled' with 'that rude kind of magnificence' which appears in 'the prospects of an open champaign country, a vast uncultivated desert, of huge heaps of mountains, high rocks and precipices, or a wide expanse of water.' Addison's papers on the 'Pleasures of the Imagination' have a directness and simplicity not always found in later philosophical speculations about imagination and beauty, and it is perhaps for this reason that they were so influential in arousing aesthetic discussion throughout the eighteenth and the nineteenth centuries. The discussion was one that ranged from theories of beauty to those of sublimity and included many volumes upon that intermediate term, the picturesque.

It was the general appeal of the picturesque and sublime between 1820 and 1850 which accounted for thousands of illustrations that appeared in the travel books, the annuals, and the periodicals of the time. That this was a golden age for such literature can in part be explained in terms of the rapid development of steam power, which facilitated travel by sea and land. Paradoxically, improved travel conditions also contributed eventually to a decline in the demand for picturesque illustration as travellers preferred to visit picturesque lands rather than read about them. Although Bartlett was to live long enough to complain about the declining interest in travel literature, it was not a serious issue for him until the 1850s. And even then the absence of photography supported a steady demand for topographical illustration. It was, therefore, a reasonably bright and tempting future which faced William Henry Bartlett shortly after he had completed his architectural training in 1829 and had agreed to provide illustrations for Dr William Beattie's projected work on Switzerland.

That Bartlett deserves biographical and critical notice today is obvious to anyone who, having studied his art or his travel books, attempts to find out more about the man. Even contemporary references to Bartlett as an artist or author rely almost entirely for their source material upon William Beattie's *Brief Memoir* (1855), which has become an extremely rare book. Because Beattie was for many years a close friend of Bartlett and had, after his death, access to the artist's journals and letters, this *Memoir* is of great importance biographically, and I have thought it wise to give it new life in the second section of this book.

My part of this work is an examination of Bartlett's art and prose in terms not only of the mid-nineteenth century and the interest in the picturesque that survived long after Wordsworth had denounced its 'rules of mimic art' but also of the twentieth century when there has been an increasing interest in Bartlett prints. Within very recent years this enthusiasm has grown noticeably. Canada's centennial celebrations, in particular, served to direct attention to its past and its pictorial records. Three publications appeared in Canada in 1967 and 1968, a facsimile edition of *Canadian Scenery*; *Bartlett's Canada, a pre-Confederation Journey*; and *Quebec 1800: A Nineteenth Century Romantic Sketch of Quebec*. It is reasonable to suppose that interest in Bartlett's travels will also expand to his records of other lands.

I must here confess the shortcomings of this book. The most grievous for me to admit is my failure to locate the many letters, journals, and other manuscript material which Beattie refers to in his *Brief Memoir*. For another omission, the rather vexed question of Bartlett's imitators, I ask to be excused on the grounds that I am not qualified to enter so technical an area. Something, too, I suppose might have been said about Bartlett scenes on Ridgway china and the remarkable prices which original pieces now fetch in reputable antique shops. This subject has, however, been dealt with quite competently by Mrs Elizabeth Collard in her recent book, *Nineteenth Century Pottery and Porcelain in Canada*, in the chapter 'Bartlett for the Table.'

A rather interesting bibliographical problem relates to the many books which appeared during and after Bartlett's lifetime bearing engravings for which he received no financial return. Many of these were published in other countries and included such works as J. Joseph Prévost, *L'Irlande au dix-neuvième siècle*

(Paris, H. Mandeville, [1845-1852]) and J.M. Wainwright, *The Pathways and Abiding-Places of Our Lord* (New York, Appleton, 1851). In England there was the very successful three-volume illustrated edition of the Holy Bible which the Virtue publishing firm brought out between 1861 and 1865. Lack of a systematic international copyright law before 1886 left authors and artists open to much shameless exploitation.

There remains now for me only to make my acknowledgments, which I do with considerable pleasure. In particular I want to thank the Canada Council for an award which enabled me to visit scenes which Bartlett sketched in Switzerland, Savoy, and northern Italy, and for a generous grant which made possible publication of this book. The Art Gallery of Ontario and the Canadiana Department of the Royal Ontario Museum have extended many courtesies to me. The removal of the Manoir Richelieu Collection of Bartlett's original work from Murray Bay to Ottawa enabled me to examine carefully eighteen of the original sketches from *Canadian Scenery* and one from *American Scenery*, which are contained in the National Archives of Canada and in the National Gallery of Canada.

I am indebted to the Victoria and Albert Museum, London, England and to the McLaughlin Library, University of Guelph, for permission to reproduce Bartlett sketches and watercolours. I have also had an opportunity to study Bartlett holdings and periodical references to his work in the British Museum. Mr William Maidment, Borough Librarian, kindly gave me permission to study The William Beattie Collection in the Central Library of the London Borough of Camden. This collection formed part of the Henry Morley Library.

Finally, I am grateful to Dr M. Elizabeth Waterston of the University of Guelph for her careful reading of the manuscript.

The symbol B000 in the text refers the reader to the appropriate page of Beattie's *Brief Memoir* reprinted in this volume.

WILLIAM HENRY BARTLETT

A Twentieth-Century View

William Henry Bartlett's place in time (1809–1854) intrudes upon two great literary periods, the Romantic and the Victorian; both of these influenced the character of his work as artist and author. Any approach to Bartlett's work requires some attention to the aesthetic and literary ideas current in his lifetime, as also to the peculiar circumstances of his life. Unwilling to sacrifice his wife and family to the cause of art, and lacking private means of his own, Bartlett was compelled to draw and to write to suit the popular taste of his time. This taste is one that cannot be easily defined despite the tremendous quantity of periodical literature of his day and the richly bound illustrated volumes that weighed down the tables and shelves in Victorian drawing rooms and libraries.

William Henry Bartlett, the second child of his parents, William and Ann Bartlett, was born in England on 26 March 1809, the day after the family had moved into the eighth house in Bartholomew Place. The house stood on the east side of Kentish Town Road not far from Bartholomew Road in today's heavily settled area of London NW 5. The house was one of eighteen double-windowed three-storey terrace homes, which adjoined another row of twelve similar ones in Trafalgar Row.[1] In 1809 the houses in Bartholomew Place were nearly new and on all sides there was open country. Years later Bartlett remembered 'its green fields ... in the soft sunshine; its tall elms ... the old familiar paths, the hedge-rows, with their well-known gaps, and flowery borders of pansies and wild violets' (B130–1). Through the elms could be seen Hampstead, Islington, and the church towers of Highgate.

Little is known of Bartlett's father. We may surmise that he belonged to the middle class for he had enough money to send William Henry to a private school and later apprentice him to John Britton, the well-known antiquarian, and to educate the younger son, Frederick Augustus, for the Anglican priesthood. This decision to place one son in orders and to article the other for seven years may well be evidence of paternal strength and decision.

Beattie's *Brief Memoir of the Late William Henry Bartlett* makes no mention of the father, but it does give a little information about the mother, Ann, who seems to have been a gentle, attractive woman whose love for her children was very real. That Bartlett's life at home was a pleasant one is obvious from his own recollection of it:

Return, ye gay holidays spent in the open fields – in green places under the shadow of the perfumed lime-trees; or the bright flowers, and broad green rustling fans of the horse-chestnuts! I can still see the stile where, on half-holidays, I was accustomed to sit, with my younger brother,[2] who came up to see me, with a little store of sweetmeats. And well do I remember the quiet afternoon, which, once a month, I spent at home – a few hours of 'fearful joy' snatched by my mother's side. And then her little treat of tea and cake; the walk back with her to school; and the choking sensation with which I received her parting kiss. (B97)

The shaping influence of the church upon William Henry was obvious, for his writings and travels in the Middle East were often motivated as much by religious as by secular interest. That this interest was fostered by his early home life appears in his memory of the pastor whose sermons first stirred his religious feelings (B131). Later in life his attitude to religion is suggestive of the early Wordsworth: 'Fair is the sunshine, soft and delicious the balmy breathing air, as on the first day of creation. My heart leaps up with the vivid joy of youth; and I embrace, too, with an instructed spirit, and adore with silent heart-worship, the eternal beauty that fills and blesses the universe.' (B131)

It is not easy to say how much credence should be given to Bartlett's condemnation of his private schooling (1816–21): 'the practice of flogging,' the wretched 'system of tuition,' the 'evil qualities in its unwholesome soil,' and 'the total deprivation of affectionate intercourse with my parents' (B96). What might have affected his future character as much as his unfortunate schooling was his own sensitive, shy temperament which his parents seem to have recognized and perhaps encouraged by indulgence at home (B96). Certainly his five years' 'immurement' at boarding school could not be compared with Coleridge's

4

at Christ's Hospital (1781–91) under the stern discipline of James Boyer.

To what degree, then, did Bartlett's schooling promote his 'morbid sensitiveness of character' (B96) which he says affected him in later life? Certainly this description of himself is quite at variance with that provided by Nathaniel Parker Willis, the American journalist, who found him, after a summer's travel in his company in 1837, 'the pleasantest of John Bulls.'³ That Bartlett could be happy and content even when absent from England and his family and when enduring the hardships of travel in the Middle East is evident in a brief passage from his diary that appears in his *Forty Days in the Desert*.⁴ Just west of Akaba at the head of the Gulf he records that he 'was undressed, and so deliciously warm and comfortable in bed, with a volume of Shakespeare in hand, and a glass of punch by [his] bedside that [he] was loath to turn out' to meet the Governor of Akaba who had just arrived. In fact, it was often his good nature and sense of humour which enabled him to accept many awkward and even disagreeable happenings on his travels: whether it was being locked in his room at 'Rays' in Alexandria;⁵ controlling the frustrating idiosyncrasies of the Bedouins in his little caravan in the Sinai Desert; choosing between the picturesque necessity of sleeping in the open air under an olive tree in Syria, and 'the interior of a khan, or private house, generally swarming with vermin';⁶ or, greatly fortified by wine and brandy, making his way on foot and at night with a party of very jolly Germans and very sober Jesuits to the summit of Mount Etna.⁷ In adventures like these the reader fails to recognize anything morose about the artist's sensibility.

Nevertheless, in later years, Beattie speaks of Bartlett's 'hours of mental depression' (B130), of his 'unremitting industry' (B136), and of 'an irritability which he struggled in vain to subdue' (B137). The reader is left with the impression that his morbidity was more closely related to his anxiety to provide adequately for his family than it was to the ill effects of his schooling. Bartlett knew that he could not expect to achieve financial independence from the commissions he received from his publisher. It is also reasonable to surmise that he knew how inferior his topographical sketches were to the watercolours of his contemporaries, of landscape artists like John Crome, Richard Bonington, John Varley, David Cox, John Sell Cotman, and, of course, J.M.W. Turner. But the popular demand for topographic illustration ensured Bartlett of an income which, if not always as bountiful as he desired, was much preferable to making such sacrifices as Samuel and Hannah Palmer endured in Italy from 1837–9, as

John Sell Cotman accepted when he went to London in 1798 and to Norwich in 1806, and as John Crome experienced between 1790 and 1803. Eventually, too, some of Bartlett's 'mental depression' may well have arisen from his own awareness of the effect which the introduction of the daguerreotype and the ever increasing ease of travel was bound to have upon the popularity of his topographical illustrations. Had Beattie been able to offer Bartlett the kind of help that Dr Thomas Monro gave artists like J.R. Cozens, Thomas Girtin, and J.M.W. Turner, the course of Bartlett's life and his achievement as an artist might have been very different.

But even accepting these arguments, it would not be prudent to overlook completely the unhappy years at boarding school. What is questionable is Beattie's statement from Bartlett's 'private memoranda' that 'the depressing influences under which the years of boyhood were passed' gradually developed 'the various propensities' of his nature and afforded 'a mimic, but too faithful image of the future man' (B96–7). This is placing too much blame upon his schooling, and neglecting and forgetting that the later 'feelings of apathy and indifference' which assailed him were more the result of his own choice of vocation than the result of 'the feeling of utter isolation and abandonment which he felt' on being immured at boarding school.

Once his schooling had ended in 1821, Bartlett came home 'for a season.' Even his mother now became concerned to place him 'out in life.' The opportunity came when a Mr Clement used his influence to put Henry (as his family called him), then thirteen, with John Britton, where he remained until he completed his apprenticeship in 1829. It was Clement, too, who was the means of Henry later meeting Dr William Beattie[8] whose intervention ensured that the young man's life as an artist was to be devoted largely to topographical illustration. That Beattie seems not to have encouraged Bartlett to undertake more imaginative work both as an artist and as an author is a reflection upon Beattie's own limitations. When he looked back, for example, at Bartlett's professional achievement in 1854, Beattie could say without qualification that his friend had won 'high and lasting distinction among contemporary artists' (B98).

II

In John Britton's establishment at 17 Burton Street in the parish of St Pancras, the boy found a friendly environment where his talents were quickly realized.

6

1 Rome [Forum Romanum; Arch of Septimius Severus and columns of Temple of Saturn]

2 Mount Etna, from the lava of 1669 *sepia wash*

Britton had followed Auguste Charles Pugin's example and had taken in pupils so that he could train them to make the sketches and architectural drawings which he needed for his 'embellished publications.'[9] Despite the occasional trouble which Henry Bartlett caused his master – 'indifference to dress, and manners, and unconquerable shyness' (B104) – the latter had good reason to be pleased with a pupil who exhibited not only 'sensibility and genius' but also 'pertinacity and self-confidence.'[10]

Britton's house was a small 'rural mansion' of three storeys divided into thirteen rooms. The first floor was below ground level. The second contained the library which was filled with shelves of practical books and drawers of prints and architectural sketches. On the same level as the library were two offices for the use of the apprentices and a small breakfast room with pictures and more sketches. The third storey contained two bedrooms, a dressing room, a sitting room, and a small octagonal cabinet room which held drawings of Celtic antiquities, portraits, and 'a small Collection of choice Books, some of which were *privately printed.*' It was the sort of room which, as Britton himself puts it, imparted 'dignified feelings to the owner.' The surrounding property, large enough for five more houses, consisted of a spacious garden with many trees and flowering shrubs and, in keeping with the author's interest in ancient monuments, an imitation Druid temple and cromlech.[11]

Here in this rural setting, close to the heart of London, Britton composed many of the forty works on topography, fine art, and architecture which bear his name. Here he took in his pupils, of whom Bartlett was the fourth, and in the course of time introduced them not only to his own antiquarian interests but also to the sketches of contemporary artists like Prout, Cotman, and Mackenzie.

According to Britton's obituary notice of Bartlett in *The Art-Journal* of 1 January 1855, the master paid a good deal of attention to the training of his pupils, and with pride he tells the readers that Henry Bartlett's 'eye and hand had been well drilled and disciplined by home experience and long practice' before any of his work was published. It is from this obituary that Beattie gets his information when he describes some of Bartlett's earliest work which was done in 1824 or 1825, the 'finished drawings of landscape' about Dorking. On this work Bartlett was accompanied by Penry Williams, who made 'four or five beautiful drawings' of the 'sumptuous apartments' of Thomas Hope's seat at Deepdene just east of Dorking. Britton notes, too, that the drawings of both artists were preserved in a folio volume at Deepdene.

7

In the training of his pupils, John Britton claims that he 'wished to create a love of Art as a mistress, and treat her attributes as handmaids. After prints, sketches, and drawings by and from the artists referred to [*sic*], they were shown what had been, and could be done by the pencil and colours; and after obtaining a knowledge of their 'ways and means – and when enabled to wield and command their own tools, they were sent into different parts of their own country to see and delineate buildings and scenes which remained in status quo.'[12] Much of the apprenticeship training was, however, architectural in nature, and Britton remarks in his obituary notice that Bartlett was required 'to make sections of the varied mouldings of arches, windows, doorways, clustered columns, and thereby tempted to understand the anatomy and constructive peculiarities of those buildings whose exterior surface his drawings were chiefly employed on.' Later the apprentice was encouraged to make elaborate drawings of English cathedrals. 'These buildings,' says Britton, 'afforded him important subjects and matter for study, not merely as illustrations of the fine and original architecture of the middle ages, but for picturesque and scenic effects ... '[13]

The only surviving letter touching upon this apprenticeship training is one which Bartlett wrote to Britton from Leeds on 2 August 1827, and now one of two letters held in the Edinburgh University library. The apprentice gives an account of his 'proceedings': he had set out from York on Saturday, 14 July for Leeds, where he left his trunk. From Leeds he went through Bradford to Skipton; by Monday he was at Bolton where he had to put up at a public house. Finding Bolton Abbey 'comparatively insignificant,' he judged it better 'to attend to the situation and scenery than to make sketches of a poor building.' The scenery on the Wharfe was 'very fine indeed,' and he spent four days in the area. He left Bolton on Saturday afternoon and walked across country to Knaresborough. Here rain prevented him from sketching and forced him to go on to Ripon where he took a lodging. Once settled in, he visited Hackfall Woods, which was near at hand, and finding that the scenery was impressive, he made a sketch of it for Britton.

Referring to Fountains Abbey, Bartlett remarks that it was 'difficult to get any view that [was] not hackneyed.' However he did 'the best [he] could, aiming at variety.' 'With respect to the Bolton Sketches,' he says, 'you will see three of [the building?] and several others of the Scenery of Fountains ... I have aimed at showing its differences and peculiarities. As there is nothing else of the kind quite similar I thought you would like the cloister – the view looking down into it struck me as being a very *characteristic* scene. I could find no good exterior views as there is no inequality in the surface.'

By Thursday 2 August Bartlett was 'anxious to reach home as soon as possible.' He intended to leave Leeds the following night or the next morning for Doncaster, where he would be 'badly off' for accommodation as it was 'the Races Time.' By the end of the next week he would be in Lincoln, where he intimated that his master had given him 'nearly a weeks work' and wished that he could 'abridge it.' He remembered having seen 'one good street scene,' but he could not 'answer for another and if 2 or 3 instead of 4 sketches of the Castle would do and the weather was favourable it [would] not detain him more than 3 days.' Remembering also that Britton had 'a sketch of Cattermoles of Lincoln,' Bartlett asked him to send it on so that he could 'examine it and make any memoranda necessary for a Drawing.' Toward the end of his four-page letter the apprentice reminded his master that living at inns was 'both expensive and un-pleasant' and that he would not have 'enough cash to forward [him] beyond Lincoln.'

Much of the interest of this letter lies in the intimate account it provides of one aspect of Britton's apprenticeship scheme, in particular, of its practical side. Throughout his letter Bartlett reveals how interested he was in picturesque scenery, the same scenery that had appealed to J.M.W. Turner when he sketched Bolton Woods and the valley of the Wharfe at various times between 1811 and 1818. Bartlett's reference to Britton's projected work for him in Lincoln relates, in all probability, to the sketches from which Britton had copper and wood engravings made to provide illustrations for his *Picturesque Antiquities of the English Cities*. Finally this letter is one which foreshadows, rather sadly, the pattern of all Bartlett's working days until his death in 1854.

One of the puzzling episodes of Bartlett's apprenticeship period is the one Beattie refers to in his *Brief Memoir* (B104–5) in which we are told of a 'fever' that Bartlett had and from which his 'recovery was long and tedious.' Beattie gives no dates for this illness, but it can be argued that Bartlett's malady and the subsequent profitable convalescence actually occurred some time in 1823 or 1824. It was late in 1823 that Bartlett's father sold 5 Bartholomew Place to Mary Wollstonecraft Shelley, who lived there from 1824 to 1829. As she may have rented part of the house before she completed arrangements for the pur-chase, it is reasonable to conjecture that the 'widow of the poet' that Bartlett

9

refers to was Mary Shelley and that it was from her books that he became familiar with 'the poems of Byron, Keats, and others' and that he first 'read of Italy and its romantic wonders – its glorious antiquities and cities, and the indescribable poetry of its climate and scenery.'

During the summer of 1829 Bartlett was in Yorkshire making studies and drawings of the ruins of abbeys including Fountains, Roche, and Rivaulx. Britton's comment on his pupil's work at this time deserves quotation: 'I have often been astonished,' he remarks, 'that he did not particularly allude to the coloured drawings he then made, as they are some of the best examples of the kind by a student in Art, I have ever witnessed.'[14] It is also astonishing that so little comment since Britton's day has been made upon Bartlett as a water-colourist. It can be explained perhaps on the grounds that very few of his water-colours exist in one place, and many of these are the sepia washes prepared for the engraver to work from. As an artist Bartlett is usually thought of in terms of the hundreds of black and white engravings of his sketches which have found their way into the hands of antique dealers and collectors throughout the western world. His reputation as a watercolourist is further diminished because so many of the engravings have been tinted to resemble watercolours. There is good cause, then, to try to discover and examine the original 'coloured drawings' which Britton referred to as belonging to the summer of 1829, for although he was very much a 'self-made' man Britton's knowledge of art was considerable.

Britton's own reputation as an antiquarian had emerged in 1807 when he published the first volume of *The Architectural Antiquities of Great Britain*, which was designed 'to elucidate the principles of ancient architecture.' By 1814 he had published three more volumes of *Architectural Antiquities*; in 1826 a fifth volume of the series appeared: *Chronological History and Graphic Illustrations of Christian Architecture in England*. This volume carries an early example of Bartlett's work in the form of a chronological study of twelve towers and spires of English churches and cathedrals. These early drawings are representational rather than imaginative and are an interesting harbinger of the qualities often associated with Bartlett's later work.

The apprentice must have been very pleased to have examples of his work appear in so handsome a volume as *Christian Architecture in England* which, we are told, owed 'its great success and popularity' to the 'superiority of its graphic illustrations'; it contained examples of the work of draftsmen like Samuel Prout, Frederick Nash, William Alexander, Thomas Hearne, John Sell Cotman, and J.M.W. Turner. It was also a volume that was extravagantly praised on the grounds 'that the successful application of the so-called "Gothic" Architecture of our ancestors to modern Ecclesiastical, and Domestic purposes, may, to a large extent, be attributed to this and other works simultaneously produced by Mr. Britton.'[15]

By the time Bartlett had signed his apprenticeship papers, his master was already deeply committed to another large work, *Cathedral Antiquities*, of which the first volume was completed by 1821 and the sixth and last volume in 1836. As with *Architectural Antiquities*, Britton stressed the value of 'correct information' and deplored the taste of 'the majority of mankind' who 'prefer the pretty to the useful; and seek rather to amuse the fancy than inform the mind.' 'Hence,' he argued, 'picturesque views, and artificial effects of light and shadow, of black and white, have been repeatedly and continually published and re-published in our antiquarian embellishments.'[16] That the pupil had to accept some of his master's enthusiasm for the useful is obvious in the Bartlett prints (1827, 1828) of Peterborough Cathedral, in those (1826, 1827, 1828, 1829) of Gloucester Cathedral, and (1830, 1831) of Bristol and Hereford cathedrals.

One of the surviving Bartlett sketches from which these engravings were made is that of 'Peterborough Cathedral, View of the Church from the N.E.' A comparison between it and the engraving (v,61) reveals at once why Britton was astonished that Bartlett ignored this and similar works. The original sketch is a charming watercolour, architecturally correct, but rich and warm with the soft English light upon the stonework. As the engraving is dated 1 April 1828, we can assume that the original watercolour may have been done in 1827 when Bartlett was just eighteen years of age. It is little wonder that Britton could praise the accuracy, style, and originality of this young man's work.

In addition to the 6 × 8 inch engravings like that of Peterborough Cathedral in *Cathedral Antiquities*, there are also vignettes taken from Bartlett sketches of Winchester, Hereford, Wells, and Peterborough which reveal Bartlett's early interest in scenery. In the one of Wells, for example, the artist's attention is taken up by the pretty and the picturesque. The cathedral spires appear in the background, but the real view is of the moat, the swans, the half-ruined tower, the Bishop's palace, the trees, and the shrubbery.

Another early work to which Bartlett, the apprentice, contributed sketches was Britton's *Picturesque Antiquities of the English Cities* published in 1830. It was 'a handsome quarto volume, containing historical and descriptive accounts of the cities, with engraved views of the gates, castles, bridges, streets, etc.'[17] In the prefatory essay to *The History and Antiquities of the Cathedral Church of Worcester*, Britton praises the *Picturesque Antiquities* as being 'the best written, and illustrated of all his works,' and also notes that it 'was the most losing speculation he ever embarked in' because the engravings were upon copper or wood rather than upon the more economical steel plates.

Of the eighty-three engravings in *Picturesque Antiquities*, Bartlett's name appears as the draftsman for sixty-seven. For many of the copper engravings John Le Keux was the engraver. They include sketches of York, Lincoln, Peterborough, Canterbury, Rochester, Winchester, Hereford, Worcester, Gloucester, Chichester, Salisbury, Wells, Bristol, Bath, and London. The dates of publication that appear on the prints cover the years 1827 to 1830 inclusive and so represent the last phase of Bartlett's apprenticeship which ended in 1829.

Most of the prints reveal Bartlett's interest in architecture, but some reveal his interest in landscape, which is particularly noticeable in the background of 'Keep Tower, Lincoln Castle,' in the pastoral elements of the foreground of 'Winchester – View of the City from the East,' and in the foreground of the 'View of the City of Bristol from s.w.' The qualities which we associate with Bartlett's later work are particularly apparent in three of the engravings, 'View of the City of Wells from the s.e.,' 'View of the City of Worcester from n.e.,' and 'View of the City of Bath from s.e.,' where landscape attracts the eye as much as the architectural features. From his viewpoint above the cities, the artist offers a wide panorama that encompasses trees, figures, and fields in the foreground, sweeps over the cities, and reveals clearly the hills and fertile valleys of the distance. Picturesque elements of topography and architecture come together effectively in these scenes.

What is always evident in the engravings and woodcuts of *Picturesque Antiquities*, however, is the quality of the training in architectural drawing which the youthful Bartlett had received from Britton. 'The View of the City of Lincoln from the South' offers an excellent illustration of the powers of his draftsmanship. Not only is his drawing of the cathedral accurate and finely done but so, too, are the houses in the foreground and the market cross. Although the pupil had taken much from the master, years later the master generously acknowledged something he had taken from his pupil. It was, Britton said, the quality of his pupil's sketches of the 'castles, bridges, old houses, bays, ruined gateways, etc.' which he had made when visiting English cities that induced him to undertake the publication of *Picturesque Antiquities of the English Cities* (B101).

Although no proof can be offered, it is possible that some of the engravings of scenes about Winchester, Southampton, and the Isle of Wight which appear in *A General History of Hampshire* may have been taken from sketches which Bartlett did when he was engaged on the work for *Picturesque Antiquities*. The *General History of Hampshire* was the work of B.B. Woodward, T.C. Wilks, and Charles Lockhart and was published (1861–9) several years after Bartlett's death.

A little-known work which contains early Bartlett engravings is *Ireland Illustrated*, published by H. Fisher, Son, and Jackson in 1831. Two other artists – G. Petrie, RHA, and T.M. Baynes – also contributed illustrations which appear two to a page and measure 4 × 6 inches. Bartlett's contribution consists of thirty-three sketches. Five of the engravings are dated 1829, twenty-four, 1830, and four, 1831, so that the original sketches were probably done during the last years of his apprenticeship when he may have travelled to Ireland on a commission from the publisher.

G.N. Wright, MA, who provided the 'Historical and Topographical Descriptions,' was professor of antiquities at the Royal Hibernian Academy. An excerpt from his Preface to *Ireland Illustrated* tells a good deal about the purpose of the book – of how, for example, the views from different counties make intelligible 'the singular wildness and peculiar character of the Irish Landscape': 'It should be observed that the Artists, engaged in the Illustrations of Ireland, were obliged to delineate, from a great variety of subjects, all of which were picturesque and sublime, landscapes representing select and distinct pieces of imagery: and the Illustrator has seized those happy occasions, for the introduction of such legends, facts, or circumstances as may well be understood by the contemplator of each scene.'

The Bartlett scenes belong to Dublin and to sites and views in the Counties of Wexford, Waterford, Cork, Kerry, and Limerick. Drawings of buildings in Dublin such as the Royal Exchange, Nelson's Pillar, St George's Church, The College of Surgeons, and the two of Trinity College are architectural drawings: correct, historically interesting, but otherwise too much the product of a young draftsman's hand to attract attention. But other Dublin scenes like the Custom House with its busy quay, the Four Courts with the bridges arching the Liffey, and the Lying-in Hospital with the street life in the foreground are clear indications of how much more interested the young artist was in a view than in a building isolated from its setting. The most interesting of the landscapes are 'Bantry House' and 'Glengariff' in County Cork. Those of Killarney are rather disappointing. Wright notes that: 'Those who have visited Glengariff ... will agree with the decision of the Illustrator, which is, that no scene, in all the concentrated beauties of Killarney, can vie with this before him, in sublimity of character, in greatness of effect, in the softer graces of the waving wood, or in the wilder rudeness of its mountain aspect.'[18] The engraving of Glengarriff shows the lake and 'picturesque' islands below with wild, encircling peaks beyond. The light is upon the centre of the scene so that the peaks and entrance from Bantry Bay are seen in a suitably romantic gloom. The records of the Royal Academy of Arts, London, reveal that in 1831 William Henry Bartlett exhibited two pictures there: one entitled 'Glen Gariff nr. Bantry,' the other 'Rivaulx Abbey.' It is rather strange that Britton never mentions this exhibition.

By 1829 Britton must have known that Bartlett was more interested in 'picturesque and scenic effects' than he was in the 'fine and original architecture of the middle ages.' *Picturesque Antiquities of the English Cities* and *Ireland Illustrated* offered many examples of the apprentice's interest in scenic effects, especially in those that could be classified as picturesque.

That Britton considered some defence necessary for a work called *Picturesque Antiquities of the English Cities* appears in his lengthy Introduction to this work:

The word *Picturesque* as applied to the antiquities of English cities ... will be clearly recognized and understood by readers who are familiar with the works of Gilpin, Alison, Price, and Knight. It has become not only popular in English literature, but as definite and descriptive as the terms grand, beautiful, sublime, romantic ... It may be loosely and indiscriminately applied – it may fail to convey clear, precise, and forcible images to some minds; but still in speaking, or writing, about scenery and buildings, it is a term of essential and paramount import. Hence it has been chosen for the title of the present work.

With all due deference to the high authority of Gilpin, whose writings teem with the feelings of the poet and the artist, I cannot approve of his compound term *Picturesque Beauty*. The words are of dissimilar import, and excite different ideas. Whilst one designates objects that are rough, rugged, broken, ruinous; the other applies to such as are smooth, clean, fresh, regular, perfect. One may be said to denote old; the other young, or new. An old, ragged, shattered tree, or building; or a piece of irriguous, broken, wild ground, with rocks, etc. are alike objects of the picturesque: whilst a young tree, a new and uniform building, a tract of smooth lawn, with flowery shrubs, may be considered and described as beautiful. In the application of these terms to the buildings of a city, I should not hesitate in calling the Bars of York, the street houses of Bristol and Coventry, *picturesque*; and the park lodges of London, with a few others of its new buildings, *beautiful*.

These two paragraphs reveal how familiar John Britton was with the theory of the picturesque in art and, in particular, with the rather slippery aesthetic of William Gilpin. It is with gentle malice that Britton quotes later in his Introduction from the passages in the *Essay on Picturesque Beauty* where Gilpin describes how a mallet instead of a chisel must be used to give picturesque beauty to 'a piece of Palladian Architecture.' But although Britton was uneasy about the precision of Gilpin's language, he was sufficiently interested in Gilpin's theories to promote a work that was to incorporate a good many of Bartlett's early sketches which obviously owed much to the popular picturesque art of the time.[19]

Britton's interest in the picturesque was largely antiquarian; in *Picturesque Antiquities* he presents, as he says, 'several interesting antient [sic] buildings, many of which are either in ruin, or so much dilapidated, as to entitle them to the appelation of Picturesque Antiquities.' Again, in the Introduction to this volume, he assures his reader that 'every castle, abbey, cathedral, fine church, and old mansion, is a monument and memento of a former age, and of former persons.' Like Antonio in the *Duchess of Malfi*, John Britton could say:

> I do love these ancient ruins.
> We never tread upon them but we set
> Our foot upon some reverend history.

Despite his objection to the lack of 'precision' in Gilpin's prose, John Britton was attracted to the picturesque and, in particular, to the idea that the 'state of ruin' that attached to ancient buildings provided the very quality of roughness which was the distinguishing feature of the picturesque. In fact, Britton trained George Cattermole, whose art reveals the influence of the picturesque, and employed Samuel Prout, who later contributed extensively to the demand for picturesque topography both in Britton's own publications and in the popular illustrated *Annuals* and travel literature of the period.[20] The apprentices at 17

Burton Street were almost certainly informed about William Gilpin's theories of the picturesque, and they may well have been encouraged to fit the theory to practice. In addition to having such knowledge, we know that they were encouraged to select and draw from the 'best specimens' of contemporary artists.[21]

Years later, during a journey from Nazareth to Tiberias, Bartlett revealed how thoroughly he had absorbed the popular taste of his day for the picturesque when he described how impressed he was by the appearance of an Arab encampment:

I was so struck with the picturesque beauty of this sudden apparition, that without a word I turned off the path, and made straight for the tents ...

The taste of Forest Gilpin or Uvedale Price could not have suggested a happier or more picturesque position than these Arabs had chosen for their temporary resting-place. The tents of the chief and his family were pitched upon a grassy ridge, gently elevated above the rest, and sheltered by some dense and wide-spreading oaks. The tents are composed of a strong coarse stuff, like sacking, woven in a broad mass of *black* relieved by a white line; and in general appearance there is little doubt they correspond with those of the earliest times. Such might have been the tent of Abraham beneath the terebinth-tree. And the figures who gathered around us were truly patriarchal in aspect; an old man, whose venerable face, with long white beard, was of a calm and benevolent expression, clothed in the broad and simple folds of his striped robe, and resting, like Jacob, on the top of his staff, surveyed us with quiet curiosity. Several others, dark in hue almost to blackness, were couched upon the ground, and regarded us from time to time from beneath the shade of their brilliant head-dresses of striped and gilt handkerchiefs, with a less pleasing expression. They might well have personified the turbulent sons of the Patriarch. We liked not the unquiet and sinister roving of their keen black eyes ... They rose and crowded round my sketch, laughing with childish delight as I transferred rapidly to my paper some traits of their primitive appearance. Their women, peeping from the tents, displayed harsh and bold faces, with the wild black eye and cunning expression of the gipsy; they were clothed in loose dresses of blue serge, gathered round the waist, and their 'posé' was noble and sculpturesque. Flocks of sheep and goats were grouped around, and horses picketed by the tent sides. All this in the heart of the forest, with the towering and woody crest of Tabor above, constituted a scene of unusual interest and beauty.[22]

The taste for the picturesque, which is so obvious in Bartlett's work, is frequently accompanied by an interest in the sublime, and it is sometimes difficult to distinguish them. Certainly the sublime, when it occurs, takes precedence over what is picturesque. Like Horace Walpole, Bartlett thrilled to sights that stirred emotions of pain or terror. His account of the Pass of Guil, in Dauphigny, as related by Beattie, is an excellent illustration:

... 'terribly grand'; rocks shattered into pinnacles, menacing the traveller with their *débris*, which is incessantly rolling down the slopes – gigantic pines blackening the sunless course of the torrent, sullenly roaring through the depths of the defile – the path insecure and precipitous – utter solitude – all conspiring to appal the traveller, and 'send forth a sleepy horror through his blood!' At a wooden bridge – the view opposite – where the narrow path descends into the dismal gorge, the scene is peculiarly savage and even sublime.[23]

It is interesting to speculate about the source of Bartlett's fascination for the sublime. The sublime was, of course, very much in fashion, so much so that its limited appeal today is one of the features that distinguishes the reports of our restless travellers from those of the early nineteenth century.

Certainly Bartlett must have discussed 'sublimities' with Beattie, who was as deeply impressed by the power of the sublime as he was by the delights of the picturesque. Bartlett would have read Beattie's account of Switzerland for which he provided the sketches. Again and again Beattie dwells upon the sublimity of the scenery, upon, for example, the Jungfrau and its glaciers as seen from the valleys of the Lütchinen : ' ... the defile of the Lütschinen, where all that is most sublime and terrific in scenery is grouped, and concentrated in a way that defies descripion. It is a pass in which the wild and powerful genius of Salvator would have revelled in kindred gloom; but even his pencil, however magical in its delineations of the Abruzzi, would here have lost half its plastic influence, and left the great master of stern and savage landscape in despair.'[24]

As described by both Bartlett and Beattie, the sublime fits on occasion rather neatly the Burkean definition. One need proceed no further than the opening sentence of Part II of *A Philosophical Enquiry into the Origins of our Ideas of the Sublime and Beautiful*, which first appeared in 1757: 'The passion caused by the great and sublime in *Nature*, when those causes operate most powerfully, is Astonishment; and astonishment is that state of the soul, in which all its motions are suspended, with some degree of horror.' This 'astonishment' comes about when the emotions are roused by sensations deriving from obscurity, power, privation, vastness, infinity, difficulty, and magnificence. To such qualities Burke attributes the source of the sublime, the 'strongest emotion which the mind is capable of feeling';[25] it is an emotion that 'operates in a manner analogous to terror' and is linked closely to 'ideas of pain and danger.'

Illustrations from Bartlett's own prose reveal links with Burke's definition of the sublime. After an exhausting and perilous climb up Etna during the night hours, Bartlett described the view over the crater at dawn: 'Vastness and dreary sublimity predominate, relieved with some few touches of exquisite beauty. Standing on the dread summit of the volcano, the eye takes in with astonishment the immense extent of the region, at once desolated and fertilized by its eruptions. Wide beds of lava – black, abrupt, and horrid – may be traced down its deep sinuosities and chasms ... and interspersed with these are broad dismal beds of ashes and scoriae – the seat of eternal desolation.'[26] One other example from *Forty Days in the Desert, on the Track of the Israelites* is perhaps enough by way of illustration. Attracted by the 'awful magnificence' and the historical association of the Serbal mountain peaks in the Sinai, Bartlett succeeded in climbing one of them which he found, in spite of his practice in the Alps, 'desperately toilsome' and dangerous, but 'fearfully sublime.' From the summit ' ... it was something grand to brood like the eagle from these all but inaccessible cliffs, over a region to which Biblical history has imparted a sublime interest, and to see, outspread like a map, the chief part of the "great and terrible wilderness," which entombed an entire generation of the Israelites ... and to behold, far-stretched-out, almost to the borders of the promised land, that great central plateau, through which their allotted period of wandering must subsequently have led them.'[27]

As obvious as the connection seems to be with Edmund Burke, it would be a mistake to argue that Bartlett's interest in the sublimities of landscape had its origin altogether in Burke's *Enquiry*, or for that matter in the writings of those more concerned with the picturesque than the sublime: William Gilpin, Uvedale Price, and Richard Payne Knight. It is more likely that Bartlett's interest in the sublime sprang from his attachment to the poets and prose writers of the Romantic period: Ramsay, Burns, Samuel Rogers, Washington Irving, Wordsworth, Coleridge, Lamb, Leigh Hunt, and Byron. On the back of a camel in the desert, for example, under 'the terrible and triumphant power of the sun,' Bartlett remembers Thomson's lines in *The Seasons*:

> All-conquering heat, oh intermit thy wrath!
> And on my throbbing temples potent thus,
> Beam not so fierce!

Bartlett's knowledge of older authors was extensive, and he can also find quotations from them to illustrate his emotions when contemplating sublime scenery. Ancient Jerusalem – 'grand, stern, and impregnable' – brings to his mind Milton's 'holy city':

> Her pile, far off appearing like a mount
> Of alabaster – tipt [*sic*] with golden spires.

Other quotations from the Bible, Cervantes, Shakespeare, Marvell, Defoe, Swift, Addison, and Gibbon slip easily into the stream of Bartlett's travel talk – often in support of the sublime or picturesque.

Another plausible source for Bartlett's interest in the sublime may well have been the tremendous attraction that the paintings of Salvator Rosa, Claude Lorrain, and Nicolas Poussin had for English artists of the eighteenth and early nineteenth centuries. The irregular, wild scenes of Rosa and the idealized landscape forms of Lorrain and Poussin provided English artists with conventions which they used again and again. Many of Bartlett's sketches reveal his reliance upon these conventions. Compare, for example, his 'Rock of Balmarussa' (*Switzerland Illustrated*, I, 37) with one of Rosa's 'Paesaggio' paintings, his 'Village of Eden' (*Syria*, I, 14) with Poussin's 'The Cascade,' and his 'Descent into the Valley of Wyoming' (*American Scenery*, I, 53) with Lorrain's 'Narcissus and Echo.' In Poussin and Lorrain the foreground is often the vantage point that offers a prospect opening between large masses of rock or trees upon some rich valley whose horizon line is varied by hills or mountains. The middleground offers up bridges and viaducts, castles and towns upon hills, and rivers and lakes whose windings add charm and depth to the perspective. It is this convention which Bartlett uses over and over again for his views. That he had unusual ability to select such prospects is obvious in many of his sketches, and this accounts in part for the many copies in oils which exist of his American scenes, especially those along the Hudson.

Salvator Rosa's influence, however, was perhaps most apparent in the picturesque landscapes of the late eighteenth and early nineteenth centuries. It is interesting that William Gilpin had nothing but praise for Salvator, who was to his mind very great 'in design and generally in composition.' According to Gilpin, Salvator Rosa was

... a man of genius, and of learning ... His style is grand; every object that he introduces is of the heroic kind; and his subjects in general show an intimacy with ancient history, and mythology ... A roving disposition, to which he is said to have given a full scope, seems to have added a wildness to all his thoughts. We are told, he spent the early part of his life in a troop of banditti: and that the rocky and desolate scenes, in which he was accustomed to take refuge, furnished him with those romantic ideas in landskip, of which he is so exceedingly fond; and in the description of which he so greatly excels. His *Robbers*, as his detached figures are so commonly called, are supposed also to have been taken from the life.[28]

In the paintings of Salvator Rosa, that man 'of genius and of learning,' Bartlett found the wild scenes of overhanging rocks and blasted trees, of stormy skies and lurking bandits, of yawning chasms and gloomy forests that worked so profound an effect upon the imagination of his contemporaries. Although much of Salvator's work is now looked upon as second rate, 'he was also,' as Sir Kenneth Clark points out, 'the inspiration of genuine poetry,' which had its effect upon the work of Alexander and John Robert Cozens and eventually upon J.M.W. Turner.[29]

That Bartlett's own knowledge of painting was extensive – if not always well informed – is obvious to anyone who reads his biography of Sir David Wilkie, *The Wilkie Gallery*, where he comments with ease upon the characteristics of such Dutch and Flemish artists as Adriaen van de Velde, Bakhuizen, Cuyp, David Teniers the younger, and Ostade. In another book, *Pictures from Sicily*, he notes the 'dull and uninviting appearance' of Civita Vecchia and remarks that only a painter in such a place could 'stave off *ennui*' for 'in the antique buildings and light houses of the port' the painter could find there 'materials for a very picturesque and Claude-like composition.'[30] Although Bartlett has more to say about the art of past centuries than of his own, he does reveal his interest in such artists of his time as Haydon, Beaumont, Lawrence, Raeburn, and William Collins. He ignores Allom, Roberts, and others who were doing work much like his own and also the watercolourists Cotman, Girtin, and Blake. Turner is mentioned, but his 'gorgeous idealities' were too far removed from picturesque landscape to evoke either praise or analysis.

The general taste for the picturesque and the sublime was apparent in painting, poetry, fiction, sculpture, architecture, and garden scenery. Common in the work of such seventeenth-century landscape artists as Lorrain, Poussin, Everdingen, and Ruisdael, it was a taste that was much in evidence long before the appearance of Gilpin's *Three Essays* in 1792. James Thomson's *The Seasons* (1726–30) and John Dyer's 'Grongar Hill' (1726) are often cited as marking 'the first step to Picturesque vision.'[31] Thomson's 'Winter' yields many evidences of the picturesque and the sublime:

> Among those hilly regions, where embraced
> In peaceful vales the happy Grisons dwell;
> Oft, rushing sudden from the loaded cliffs,
> Mountains of snow their gathering terrors roll.
> From steep to steep, loud-thundering, down they come,
> A wintry waste in dire commotion all;
> And herds, and flocks, and travellers, and swains,
> And sometimes whole brigades of marching troops,
> Or hamlets sleeping in the dead of night,
> Are deep beneath the smothering ruin whelmed.

Such description can serve as the introduction to many of the sketches which Bartlett made for *Switzerland Illustrated* to impress upon the readers the perils of travel along the gorge of the Via Mala in the Grisons or of avalanches overwhelming French troops passing the Splügen on their way to Marengo.

The Salvator Rosa elements that William Gilpin so admired are nearly always present, 'peculiarly savage and sublime': ruined towers, waterfalls, cleft rocks, blasted trees, caves, mountains, cliffs, and views into winding, narrow valleys. It is no accident that more than forty prints in *Canadian Scenery* have gnarled and broken trees in the foreground and that at least thirty-two of the prints have one, or two, or three lone figures sometimes leaning over a great chasm, sometimes lurking in a forest opening, or, on occasion, perched perilously on a great, jagged rock as in the scene of 'Split Rock' on the St John River (*Canadian Scenery*, II, 105).

Spiked by a generous measure of sublimity, the picturesque provided Bartlett with a popular artistic tincture whose base had been carefully prepared from the dry compound of architectural drawing in his training from 1822 to 1829. The tincture was all the more acceptable because it appealed to the general critical taste of the time. These were the years that bore witness to so much outgoing of the Romantic spirit in English literature: to the publication, for instance, of Byron's *Don Juan, The Miscellaneous Poems of Wordsworth* in four volumes, Hazlitt's *Table Talk, Adonais, Elia,* and of the romantic fiction of Sir Walter Scott.

21

III

In 1829, after 'several weeks amidst the monastic ruins of Yorkshire,' the young Bartlett took leave of John Britton and moved out a little uncertainly to meet the requirements of one or two publishing houses in Victorian England. But, long before he could realize just how precarious was the vocation he had chosen, Bartlett was able, supported largely by the endowments of a romantic age, to earn a livelihood for himself, his wife, and his five children, to travel very extensively in the old world and the new, and to leave more visible signs of his art than did many of his talented contemporaries.

Sometime in 1830, or early in 1831, Henry Bartlett met Susanna Moon, two years his junior and niece of the Lord Mayor of London, courted her, and married her on 6 July 1831. How difficult the courtship was for a young man so morbidly sensitive, shy, and retiring, as he maintained he was, we can only guess. It is Beattie, his biographer, who says that Henry and Susanna spent a honeymoon of one month with a relation in Holland during which time there was a ten-day trip up the Rhine. On their return to London, Henry 'fixed his residence in his native suburb' and 'resumed his connection with his publisher' (B105), George Virtue, whom he had met through the intervention of John Britton.

With the exception of a period from May 1840 to March 1841 at Ramsgate, Bartlett's family always resided in the Kentish Town district. Sometime early in 1846 'for the benefit of his health' the artist took 'a small house in Highgate' at 17 Wood Lane, where the 'view which it commanded over the richly wooded flats of Essex, the picturesque environs of Hornsey, Hampstead, and other scenes of classic celebrity, was quite to his taste' (B129). That Bartlett moved his residence more than once during his life is obvious from headings on letters which he wrote to Beattie. Two of them bear the address of Trafalgar Place; two of 9 Trafalgar Place where he was living in October 1843; one of 37 High Street, Camden Town; and one just of Kentish Town. None of these letters is dated.

What Beattie has to say about Bartlett's family relationships in his *Brief Memoir* is altogether to Bartlett's credit. There is a good deal of evidence to suggest that, despite his many prolonged absences abroad, he proved to be a devoted husband and a responsible father to five children: John Spencer (born in 1835), Frederick Henry (1836), [these two dates may be misleading as they are calculated from age at death] Anne Susan (1839), Thomas Lemon (1843),

3 View from Boston Tower [England] *sepia wash*

4 The Piraeus *steel engraving*

and Helen (1848). At the end of 1832 his bride accompanied him to Switzerland where she nursed him through a serious illness. In 1834 she went with him as far as Naples and then returned alone to England. In 1840 Beattie says that Bartlett took his family to Ramsgate where he stayed for the autumn and winter in the village of St Lawrence 'sedulously attending to the health and education of his children' (B124). The description which Beattie gives of Bartlett with his family at Highgate in 1846 reveals the man's concern for his children's education: 'His leisure was chiefly filled up with parlour lessons to the little group, whose health, and progress in the rudiments of education, were the objects of his daily and hourly solicitude. And when these were concluded, a ramble in the adjoining wood, or on Hampstead Heath, was the usual reward of diligence and good conduct' (B130). On two occasions the father took one of his boys with him on his travels: once to the Mediterranean in 1850 and again to Switzerland in 1853.

Bartlett's solicitude for the health of his children was such that Beattie felt compelled to comment upon it as an indication of 'the extreme sensibility of his nature.' Whenever 'any serious illness invaded the family,' Beattie noted that the father's 'entire devotion to the object, and disregard for all personal convenience and comfort, were such as I have rarely witnessed in the course of my long experience' (B137).

Between the time his apprenticeship ended in 1829 and his marriage in July 1831, Bartlett had continued to do journeyman work for John Britton. Many of the Bartlett engravings in *Picturesque Antiquities* bear the dates 1829 and 1830. In addition to this work and that of *Ireland Illustrated*, he gained employment sketching views for *The Watering Places of Great Britain and Fashionable Directory*, which was published by I.T. Hinton in 1831 and dedicated to 'His Most Gracious Majesty William IV.'

The seventeen Bartlett views in *The Watering Places* are of south coastal resorts such as Ramsgate, Rottingdean, Brighton, Worthing, Bognor, Hastings, and Dover. These usually show the esplanade, the new hotels built to attract the aristocracy to the coast, and such picturesque prospects as the rocky coast at Hastings or the cliffs and castle of Dover; in Brighton the view is of the Pavilion and statue of George IV. The illustrations accompany a detailed description of the history and tourist attractions of the various 'watering places.' As with many of the books in which Bartlett prints appear, however, the accompanying text is

23

so inferior to the prints that booksellers have seldom hesitated to destroy the text for the sake of the Bartlett scenes. *The Watering Places* was a sort of tourist guide for the *beau monde* of William IV's day which, among many other things, informed the readers that the Royal Baths at Worthing ' ... which occupy an elegant and very conspicuous mansion in the western part of the Esplanade, are conducted by their spirited proprietor, Mr. Thomas Palmer, under whose management no arrangement which can possibly conduce to convenience or comfort has been neglected. Amongst its most important features is the complete separation of the two suites of baths; that for the gentlemen being on the ground, and the one for ladies on the first-floor, with a waiting-room attached to each; there are additional step baths for the accommodation of invalids; and the Indian medicated vapour, the douch, the shower, and every other description of bath recommended by the faculty.'[32]

In 1832 John Britton and E.W. Brayley published *Devonshire and Cornwall Illustrated* to which Bartlett contributed fifteen sketches for the Devonshire section. The Preface to this section reminds the readers that Devon's 'natural scenery is of the highest order of sublimity and magnificence, combined with every delightful variation of romantic and beautiful combination that can either charm the eye or interest the imagination.' The volume is another of the many which reveal the extensive interest there was in picturesque and topographical illustration at the beginning of Victoria's reign.

Bartlett's first major undertaking was to provide illustrations for *The History and Topography of the County of Essex*, of which the first volume appeared in 1831 and the second in 1835. They contain eighty-six Bartlett prints, most of which represent sketches made in 1831 and 1832 and a few in 1833. The prints reveal many charming views and prospects of villages and towns, of shire halls, churches, abbeys, ruins, lodges, castles, and of the kind of country homes which so interested Jane Austen's Mrs Bennet.

Several of the country houses like Hare Hall (II, 446), completed in 1769, display their Georgian style façade rather starkly across the treeless grounds; others like Terling Place (I, 139), whose grounds had been 'greatly improved by the last and present proprietor,' appear part of an 'extensive and pleasant' prospect owing much to tastes established by Lancelot Brown. What Bartlett thought of the architectural merits of the more recent country homes is unknown. His task was really to ensure that pictorial prominence was given to the possessions of the 'persons and families' in Essex whose names were listed in the index, for these would be the people whom Thomas Wright could expect to buy his handsome *History and Topography of the County of Essex*.

Of more general interest in these volumes are the few prints that reveal scenes of village streets, those that blend architecture and landscape, and those that are just landscape. Such village scenes as Thaxted (II, 234), Chipping Ongar (II, 328), Saffron Walden (II, 105) show too how much more easily and naturally Bartlett sketched buildings than he did people; his figures in the streets seem wooden and seldom really a part of their environment. Indeed, landscape always contributes far more than figures to his later sketches, even as it does in 'Chingford Church, Essex' (II, 472) in which the sunken road and the towering trees assume greater importance than the figures on the road or the small ghostly figure in the graveyard. In a few prints such as 'Hadleigh Castle Looking Towards Sheerness' (II, 598), 'Scene from Laindon Hall, near Horndon' (II, 574), and 'Wivenhoe, Essex' (I, 394), extensive views of rural and coastal scenery suggest the kind of work that Bartlett was to do for numerous travel books throughout the rest of his life.

It is interesting, for example, to place the print of 'Manningtree' (II, 781) in Essex alongside that of 'Hallowell' (Picton) in *Canadian Scenery* (I, 104), a scene Bartlett sketched six years later when he visited the Bay of Quinte in Ontario. The two pictures show surprising similarities: the tree at the left, the prospect created by the water and the indented shoreline, the village in the right middleground of the illustration, the figures in the foreground, and the low hills in the background. It is really impossible to see any change of technique in the two pictures; it is a technique that applies to scores of Bartlett's later sketches made to meet the early Victorian demand for picturesque topography.

By the spring of 1832 Bartlett's talents as an artist were more obvious than his chances of employment. He must, therefore, have thought himself fortunate when he met Dr William Beattie, who proposed that he should do the illustrations for his book on Switzerland. Beattie at this time was thirty-nine years of age, a graduate in medicine in 1818 from the University of Edinburgh; for fourteen years, 1822–36, he served as physician to the Duke of Clarence, later William IV of England. In this capacity he had accompanied the Duke and Duchess on their visits to Germany in 1822, 1825, and 1826 and had travelled extensively in that country. By 1832 he had a well-established medical practice in Hampstead and a penchant to be known as a man of letters. His *Journal of a Residence in Germany* had appeared in 1831; two years later he published a poem in cantos: *The Heliotrope, or, Pilgrim in Pursuit of Health*. In the same year he was introduced to Lady Blessington, the well-known London hostess.

In 1833 Lady Blessington lived in Seamore Place in Park Lane, London; her home had been decorated and elaborately furnished under the guidance of the gay and irresponsible Alfred D'Orsay.[33] Here the Countess entertained such well-known figures as George Colman, Samuel Rogers, Thomas Campbell, Samuel Carter Hall, Edward Bulwer Lytton, and the Earl of Durham. After he had been accepted at Seamore Place, Dr Beattie was often invited to Lady Blessington's dinners and, according to the *Dictionary of National Biography*, remained 'her very useful friend,' contributing poems to her *Book of Beauty* and other *Annuals*.

It was a year later in May 1834 that the young American man of letters, Nathaniel Parker Willis (1806–1867), who contributed the literary parts of *American Scenery*, *Canadian Scenery*, and *The Scenery and Antiquities of Ireland*, met Lady Blessington and was captivated enough by her charms to ensure that comings and goings at Seamore Place appeared frequently in his dispatches published in *The New York Mirror*. Willis may have met Beattie at Seamore Place in 1834, but we do know that in August 1835 Beattie attended Willis when he was ill of a fever in London. The two men must have talked about their publishing projects. Certainly Willis must have heard of *Switzerland Illustrated*, for Beattie would then have been busy on the letter press that was to accompany the Bartlett illustrations which had already been completed. As Bartlett was in the Middle East throughout much of 1834 sketching for Carne's *Syria, the Holy Land, Asia Minor etc.*, it was probably in 1835 that he met Willis and talked to him about an 'extensive work, to be called the *Scenery of America*.' Beattie attributes the idea to Willis, whom he says he had 'the pleasure of introducing to Mr Bartlett' (B118). But, however it happened, it is fair to say that the social amenities of Seamore Place helped promote the necessary friendships.

As Beattie indicates in his *Memoir* of Bartlett (B106), 'the popular taste for illustrated works' was at this time 'on the increase,' and there was reason to think 'that the more striking scenes of Helvetian landscape, if well painted and described, would be no unwelcome boon to the British public.' Certainly there was nothing unusual about Beattie's proposal. English travellers and artists had been crossing Switzerland and visiting that country in increasing numbers from the seventeenth century. Geneva was a popular resting place for those on the

26

'Grand Tour' in the eighteenth century. By the beginning of the nineteenth century, early English watercolourists like Alexander Cozens, Francis Towne, William Pars, John Sell Cotman, and John Mallord William Turner had sketched scenes on the continent from Normandy to Naples. In 1829 William Callow was in Paris preparing engravings for an illustrated book on Switzerland. J.F. Lewis visited the Tyrol and Switzerland before he went to Spain in 1832. Another of the English watercolourists, David Roberts, travelled in Spain and Morocco (1832–3)[34] and in Egypt and the Holy Land (1838–9) 'making everywhere numerous sketches of architecture and Eastern life.'[35]

The popularity of travel pictures is apparent in the *Annuals* that appeared after 1820. Engraving on steel, instead of copper, contributed much to ensuring that thousands of people became vividly aware of the romantic possibilities of travel, which were so greatly facilitated by the growth of steamships and railways after 1830. When Henry Bartlett left with his bride for Paris and Switzerland in November 1832, there already was a public with a pronounced taste for illustrated travel books and a publisher, George Virtue, willing to take necessary risks and promote sales.

As *Switzerland Illustrated* was to be a work 'more ostensibly devoted to the "sublime and picturesque"' than to the 'moral features of Switzerland,'[36] Bartlett found himself with employment which was very much to his liking, as sections in Beattie's *Memoir* indicate: 'How find words to convey an idea of those wondrous Alps, soaring above plain and lake, and successive mountain ranges, into the serenity of a loftier heaven?' (B108) After a spell of serious illness in which he was well cared for by his wife, the young artist set to work. 'His sketches were finished on the spot, sent home to the publisher, and placed in the hands of the engraver so that the several processes of sketching, engraving, and printing, were all going forward at the same time.' (B110)

Bartlett's relations with his engravers seem not to have been close. As with his Swiss work, the finished sketches were often sent to Virtue in England, and Virtue then handed them to the engravers. In a letter to Beattie (6 June 1835), Bartlett says that he did not receive word in Turin from Wallis (perhaps R. Wallis whose name appears under twenty of the engravings in *Switzerland Illustrated*). In another letter to Beattie, which is undated, Bartlett observes that Virtue had told him privately that Wallis did not often visit him. That Bartlett was concerned about the engraving of his sketches is obvious also in his

27

letter to Beattie from Lausanne (21 March 1833) in which he says: 'I can only hope that we shall be fortunate in the Engraving. Knowing how Mr. V[irtue] is beset by a large connection, I confess I am not a little apprehensive.'

As he continued to do throughout the remaining twenty-two years of his life, Bartlett travelled a great deal and sketched quickly. According to Beattie the first number of *Switzerland Illustrated* appeared less than four months after his arrival in the country. The two volumes, containing 108 Bartlett engravings, were published in 1836, and were dedicated 'most respectfully' to 'Her Gracious Majesty, Adelaide, Queen of Great Britain and Ireland etc.'

As it has done for many artists, Switzerland offered Bartlett a startling variety of landscapes and, in particular, those which stirred the emotions to wonder and astonishment. Beyond Martigny, on the road to Chamounix, he stopped so that he could draw the rocks and wild heights of the Tête Noire looming far above the brawling waters of the Trient. The sketch was an impressive one and the resultant engraving must have delighted the publisher as he thought of its appeal to readers whose fondness for romantic adventure novels or whose own travel experiences required just this kind of engraving to help them recall literary and pictorial landscapes they had known.

Although lacking the artistic merit of Alexander Cozens' 'Rainstorm over Mountains,' the younger Cozens' 'Pays du Valais,' or Francis Towne's 'Source of the Arveiron,' Bartlett's sketches of Switzerland offer an extremely interesting topographical and historical record of his travels. Unlike Town's treatment of the Mer de Glace and the black peak beyond it, or the hazy distances of J.R. Cozens' 'Pays du Valais,' Bartlett's sketches nearly always reveal his concern for detail, his love of buildings, and his interest in the men and women and animals that he found so difficult to sketch effectively.

On more than one occasion Bartlett's sepia sketches for the engraver seem to have become detailed watercolours in which the artist tried to reveal the varied colouring as well as the topographic details of the view. One such watercolour is a scene over Sion in Switzerland down the Rhone valley to the mountains beyond; the landscape corresponds closely to that in 'Ruins of the Episcopal Palace, Sion' (*Switzerland Illustrated* I, 47), but in this original the figures of the engraving are missing and the trees in the foreground are quite different. It may be, of course, that Bartlett did two sketches of this scene, one in sepia and one in watercolour, and that the sepia is now lost. That this may be so could be concluded from the comparatively large size of the watercolour (11 × 8 inch; the sepias

28

from which the engraver worked were usually 5 × 7 inch). The delicate soft colours in the original and the loving attention that the artist gave to the ancient buildings make this a charming picture of one of the best-known views in the Rhone valley. The pencil lines and the mountain peak at the top right indicate that the watercolour is unfinished or intended only for the engraver.

Only 21 of the 108 sketches in *Switzerland Illustrated* lack buildings of any kind. In all the others, bridges, churches, castles, monasteries, towers, forts, and municipal buildings are much in evidence. Nor is the interest merely antiquarian. Only about a dozen prints of ancient buildings or ruins appear. It is seldom that the scene is not enlivened by small groups of people – peasants, tourists, the military, or the clergy – often shown at their daily round: boating, carting, fishing, faggot gathering, herding, tending vines, travelling, seeking shelter, haymaking, taking part in religious processions or in village jollifications. Only in a limited sense can these people be thought of as *banditti* for there is nothing sinister about most of them. The lone figure that stands looking at the Aar Fall at Handek, for example, could be Bartlett's sketch of himself, for he had good reason to remember his attempt to make the passage of the Grimsel:

Being informed that it was perfectly practicable, he set out early, and, proceeding alone, spent some time at the cascade of the Aar, near Handek. From that point where the ascent is very wild – particularly so at this season (May, 1835), when the snow of the avalanches lay unmelted, and arching the torrent of the Aar, which had eaten its way through the enormous masses precipitated during the winter – he arrived at length at the last bridge over the torrent, which, being greatly swollen by the melting snows, foamed over loose blocks of granite – forming an almost continuous cataract ... He had mounted to about 40 or 50 feet above the river, when having some doubts as to the path, and remaining some moments to survey the locality, he determined to descend. He had scarcely done so ... when the sound of a rushing avalanche from above burst upon his ear, and looking up he beheld with consternation a *débris* of large snow blocks bursting over the summit of the slope and descending upon him with impetuosity ... he was dashed headlong ... into the rushing torrent beneath. Stunned by the crash, he recovered only to what appeared certain destruction ... he struggled to gain the bank ... and clung for support to a projecting rock overhanging the torrent ... By renewed exertion, however, he succeeded in scrambling along the rugged rocks overhanging the stream ... and thus effected his escape. Had he been carried down only a few yards further, he must have perished, as the stream at that point makes a sudden leap over a precipice ... Sensible that a sudden chill from the snow-water was to be dreaded, he retraced his steps ... to Handek, and

29

thence to Guttanen,[37] where at nightfall he entered the small inn, went instantly to bed, and by promoting perspiration with tea and other warm liquids, succeeded in preventing any serious results.[38]

It may well be that Bartlett's early training under Britton accounts for his not giving way entirely to the vogue for the picturesque and especially to Beattie's fondness for the sublime. As Beattie looked at the glaciers of Grindelwald, he regretted that he had 'nothing with which to compare the scene,' nothing 'to give it that vivid colouring' so that 'those who have not had ocular demonstration may recognize its wild phenomena':

From the windows of the inn the eye wanders over the more striking features of the scene. Below, the torrent descends with thundering precipitation from its source in the icy cavern, the opening to which forms a magnificent arch of seventy feet in height. Above, the glacier split into towers and pinnacles, and sparkling with the sun, merges its sea-green ramparts in a wilderness of everlasting snows. The pinnacles, so well known under the name of horns or aiguilles, present an appearance the most unprecedented to the eye and mind of a stranger. One of these, a tremendous obelisk, shooting its precipitous and tapering form to nearly twelve thousand feet, fringed at its base with forests, and encrusted with snow, exerts a sort of fascination over the senses, and holds the spectator for a time in mute and breathless contemplation.[39]

But a study of Bartlett's sketch, 'The Village of Grindelwald' (II, 98), reveals that he was as much, if not more, interested in the architectural detail of the inn and the life in the street than he was in the glacier and the towering mass of the Wetterhorn, which appears like a theatre backdrop in his picture. The inn, now called 'Gasthof Steinbock Grindelwald,' is so carefully drawn that today's tourist has no difficulty distinguishing it from the others on the same street. This careful attention to architectural and topographical detail characterizes Bartlett's work and helps account for the continuing popularity of his work. Of course, it may be argued that he saw in the 'Gasthof' something picturesque, but this quality is controlled, as it were, by Bartlett's faithful representation of the scene. Unlike William Gilpin's, his views are easily defined in terms of place.

In his letter written to Beattie from Lausanne, 21 March 1832, Bartlett explains that he has so arranged his route as 'to omit nothing of popular interest' in Switzerland; he is also 'persuaded' that his collection of sketches 'will prove characteristic of her sublime scenery.' He remarks that he is much pleased with

Lake Leman, but it is 'of too extended a cast to be strikingly picturesque.' The eastern part of the lake 'including Vevey, Chillon, and Meillerie appears very beautiful.' It is a letter which reveals his concern for 'striking subjects,' his regret that he cannot visit Schaffhausen and that he must obtain a sketch of the falls from an English portfolio, his apprehension lest Virtue not provide skilled engravers for his drawings, and his gratitude to Beattie for having originated the project. It is finally a letter that indicates how much Bartlett was attracted to both the picturesque and the sublime.

Before *Switzerland Illustrated* was ready for publication, Bartlett was in Alexandria on his way to the Holy Land where he was to draw the 107 sketches that make up the illustrations in the three volumes of John Carne's *Syria, the Holy Land, Asia Minor*. In 1826 John Carne, who had travelled extensively in the Middle East in 1821 visiting Constantinople, Greece, Egypt, and Palestine, published *Letters from the East*, a book which Bartlett must have known and found useful when he was preparing the illustrations for *Syria, the Holy Land, Asia Minor*. The Middle East was a very popular subject, and a publishing firm like Fisher's would be quick to realize the advantage of an illustrated book on the subject as compared with Carne's *Letters* which had, however, run to three editions with only one illustration, the frontispiece.

Between 1790, when James Bruce's *Travels to Discover the Source of the Nile* appeared, and 1818, when Edward Daniel Clarke's eight volumes on *Travels in Various Countries of Europe, Asia and Africa* were published, more than twenty noteworthy travel books about the Near and Middle East were placed before the public. Napoleon's conquest of Egypt and his disastrous campaign in Syria had attracted considerable attention to the East even as Byron's travels and poetry, a decade later, stirred romantic imaginings about Turkey, Greece, and the Levant. The interrelationships of Muhammed Ali, Sultan Mahmud, and Tsar Nicholas also guaranteed that, politically, western Europe had to remain alert to happenings at the eastern end of the Mediterranean. And, of course, the building of railways in France and the introduction of the steamship greatly facilitated travel to the Middle East.

Though these were strong influences on western travellers, it is questionable, in Bartlett's case, if any affected him more than the religious one. His detailed knowledge of the scriptures and of biblical history is apparent throughout his writing. He wanted to see the lands of the Old and New Testaments as much for his own sake as he did for the sketches commissioned by George Virtue in

London. Like H.V. Morton in our time, he was fascinated by St Paul's life and journeys, which he retraced by much the same means as the Apostle himself had used. Jerusalem, for William Henry Bartlett, was a sacred city. The emotions which his approach at dawn to Jerusalem awoke within him do much to explain the six visits which he paid to the Middle East: 'I had stood,' he remarks, 'alone within the awful circle of the Coliseum, when faintly touched by the light of the rising moon, and had watched the lunar rainbow spanning the eternal foam which rises from the base of Niagara; but this nocturnal approach to the ancient capital of Judea, across her bleak and desolate hills, awoke a more sublime and thrilling emotion. The walls of that city, the scene of events which must ever remain the most touching in their influence upon the human heart, which I had so long and earnestly hoped to see, were, after one disappointment, at length at hand.'[40]

Like Beattie, John Carne was impressed by the vividness of Bartlett's letters and quotes directly from them in *Syria, the Holy Land, Asia Minor* when he describes Djouni, the residence of Lady Hester Stanhope. Bartlett's account here has a kind of immediacy that is lacking when he describes the same event some sixteen or seventeen years later in his own book, *Footsteps of Our Lord and His Apostles*. In his earlier account he remarked:

I, who had expected a crabbed imperious old woman, was most agreeably surprised by the noble but gentle aspect of our strange hostess. In youth she must have been most beautiful: her features are remarkably fine, blending dignity and sweetness in a fascinating degree. Her dress was fantastic, but impressive: her turban of pale muslin shadowing her high pale fore-head. There is certainly a slight vein of fitful insanity in her expression, but its general and ordinary cast is that of one calmly persuaded of the truth of principles reposed on with deep satisfaction. She conducted us to an arbour in the gardens, quite English in appearance. I made this observation, when she replied, 'Oh, don't say so; I hate everything English!' Then nodding to my companion, who was an American, 'he has a good star – very good': then addressing herself to me, 'You are of a cheerful disposition, see everything *en couleur de rose*; one of those beings who pass well through life. You will rise about the middle of your life. You are apt to be violently angry on occasion, and I *could* let out more.'[41]

In contrast with this passage are corresponding accounts which Bartlett wrote for *Footsteps of Our Lord and His Apostles*. Lady Hester here becomes a person ' ... certainly possessed – partly, no doubt, from nature, but principally from long and penetrating habits of observation – an almost preternatural power of

32

divining the characteristics of those subjected to her gaze, especially those least obvious to the common observer, but of which the conscience of the startled delinquent secretly recognized the truth.'[42] The interview in the arbour comes out this way in *Footsteps*: 'Satisfied apparently by her scrutiny that my star was neither hostile nor malignant, she led the way into her garden, struck with the beauty of which, the fresh green of its turf and alleys, kept, especially for so sultry a climate, in the nicest order, I could not help remarking that it reminded me of England. This remark, though it might afford a secret pleasure, was by no means graciously received. "Don't say so," she exclaimed; "I detest everything English"; yet the semblance of this feeling with which she was so often reproached, was no doubt but the affected hatred expressed by many when disappointed in gaining an object secretly beloved.'[43]

Several of the engravings in *Syria, the Holy Land, Asia Minor*, deserve notice. The 'Fall of the River Cydnus' (I, 8) is a very attractive sketch with the waterfall in the foreground and snow-crested Mount Taurus in the background; 'The Ruins of Balbec' (I, 11) and the 'Gothic Castle in a Valley near Batroun' (I, 45) illustrate perfectly one aspect of the picturesque. 'A Turkish Divan – Damascus' (I, 12), the 'House of Girgius Adeeb, at Antioch' (I, 56), 'Halt of a Caravan in the Desert Plains of Girgola' (II, 49), and the 'Port of Beirout' (III, 64) reveal clearly how interested Bartlett was in the lives and customs of the Eastern people. These interests are often linked with contrasting ones set against the history of the land, as when the artist writes of what he saw as he sketched the Convent of Mount Carmel: 'As I stood ... at the farthest extremity, the light glancing through the half-closed gate, the contrasted features of the Dervise keeper, of the Catholic monks and their European guests, the picturesque Arabs and Armenians, formed a strange sight: all were gathered with reverence on the spot sacred to the recollection of Elijah. From its portal we saw, at the foot of the promontory, the narrow path which Paul must have traversed in his journey from Ptolemais to Cesarea.'[44]

Between 2 January 1834, when Bartlett and his wife had left England for Naples, and 6 July 1835, when Bartlett expected to return a second time to England, much had happened. We can only guess, however, at what he and Susanna did in Naples. It is very likely that they visited Pompeii and that they spent as much as two months in the area because Bartlett did not arrive in Beyrout until 15 June 1834. On his way he was delayed for some time in Malta and had also to spend three weeks in quarantine in Alexandria. Probably he did not part from Susanna until late March or early April, in which case she might very well, as Beattie says, have reached Lyons by 13-14 April when 'the revolution was at its height.' She may have been pregnant at the time, for her first child was almost certainly born before her husband returned from Syria to England in January 1835. It is also reasonable to believe that Bartlett may have done some sketching while he was in Naples with Susanna, and that the drawings of Naples, Sorrento, and Salerno – engravings of which appear in George N. Wright's *The Shores and Islands of the Mediterranean* and *The Rhine, Italy and Greece* – belong to this period.

Early in April 1835, Bartlett left Susanna a second time to travel in the country of the Waldenses in Piedmont and Dauphiny, beginning at Turin and ending at Grenoble. On this journey he prepared sketches for Beattie's book on the Waldenses. Bartlett's experiences among the Protestants of Piedmont and Dauphiny give us an intimate view of the artist; from his diaries and letters Beattie obtained first-hand information, for example, about the 'primitive Christians' who lived at Brunissard near the Col d'Izoarde in Dauphiny. Some of his information he quotes at length in *The Waldenses* and in abbreviated form in the *Brief Memoir*. The quotations reveal Bartlett's humanity, his power of observation, and his deep interest in the welfare of those who accepted him in their rude homes and gave him as food their different cheeses and 'the hard rye-bread of the country.' With Pastor Ehrman he entered one of the 'miserable hovels':

on opening the door, a close foetid odour almost stifled me. It seemed as if we were plunging into Cimmerian darkness, and I involuntarily shrunk back. 'Never mind – a little further – a few steps' – said my reverend conductor; and, taking me by the arm, we proceeded, my feet sinking at every step into a sub-stratum of accumulated manure and litter. Here the tinkling of bells and the breathing of cattle soon explained the character of the habitation; and presently my eyes becoming more accustomed to the light, I fairly discovered the stalls and mangers occupied by the cattle. At the extremity, a Rembrandt-like picture presented itself; the half light struggled through a narrow smoke-blackened aperture upon the squalid inhabitants of this hovel, grouped in a circle, and occupied in spinning. Their beds, like a ship's cabin, were ranged on either side; and I was surprised to observe that the ornamental details were very tolerably carved.

At a religious gathering soon to follow, Bartlett found the scene 'too remarkable ever to be forgotten': 'the pastor ... addressed his hearers in a short forcible exhortation. I have heard and read many such, but never listened to a more evangelical, and at the same time practical, address. The style was simple and familiar, and, at the conclusion, extremely touching. This little gathering together of God's people departed slowly, again to resume that life of toil and industry which is only interrupted by the intervals of prayer and of needful rest.'[45]

By 6 June 1835 Bartlett had completed this assignment and was in Martigny, Switzerland, having just crossed over the Great St Bernard on his way to the Gemmi Pass and Schaffhausen. In a letter which he wrote to Beattie at this time he detailed instructions on how to travel through Piedmont and Dauphiny; it is fairly obvious that Beattie's *Waldenses* owed a great deal to Bartlett. In 1836 Beattie himself followed much the same route as Bartlett suggested and drew extensively upon the source books that Bartlett recommended in his letter: W.S. Gilly's *Narrative of an Excursion to the Mountains of Piedmont ...* published in 1824 and his *Memoir of Felix Neff* published in 1832, Alexis Muston's *History of the Vaudois*, Jean Leger's *General History of the Evangelical Churches in the Valleys of Piedmont*, and Henri Arnaud's *Glorious Recovery by the Vaudois of their Valleys*. In addition to reminding Beattie of the importance of these books, Bartlett gave him the names of leading Waldensian pastors like Alexis Muston at Bobbi; warned him that 'the Inns in the High Alps and Vallies are but so, so, except at La Tour'; told him where he could find guides, although admitting he had had none himself; and made certain that Beattie's tour embraced 'the chief points of interest on both sides of the Alps.'

Although details are not available, the letter is interesting also because of Bartlett's reference to some kind of dissatisfaction about *Switzerland Illustrated*: 'I deeply regret the occurrence of any *sort* of complaint of the last Nos. of Switzerland and in particular that any sort of misunderstanding should exist between the parties concerned. I can only say, in the absence of particulars, that I can *scarcely* doubt but that perfect harmony will be restored – and for myself that the views I am now engaged in shall not if possible exhibit any falling off.' The Bartlett 'views' in *The Waldenses* are certainly as effective as those in *Switzerland Illustrated*. There is the same close attention to architectural detail and topography, the same interest in the picturesque landscape. Indeed in his Preface Beattie maintains that *The Waldenses* is a book very largely 'devoted to the Picturesque.'

Of the seventy-one steel engravings in *The Waldenses*, thirty-five are from sketches which Bartlett made as he travelled about in the Protestant valleys of

Piedmont and Dauphiny. His views of Pomaret, Bobbi, Fenestrelle, and the Col de la Croix (*Waldenses*, pp. 73, 33, 70, 48) must have pleased the taste of his time: bridges over torrents, jagged rocks, broken walls, prospects of mountain valleys – for those who liked the picturesque; towering mountain ranges beyond Château Queyraz in the Valley of the Guil (*Waldenses*, p. 192), the horrors of a *tourmente* on the Col de la Croix, impregnable fortresses barring mist-shrouded valleys and gorges – for those who preferred sublimity.

As in *Switzerland Illustrated*, Bartlett's scenes of Piedmont and Dauphiny are faithful representations, although not always as exact as his drawing of the Victor Emmanuel Bridge in Turin with the Mother of God Church and the hills in the background (*Waldenses*, p. 15). For such work the years of apprenticeship with Britton served Bartlett well indeed. Other scenes are not so easily identified because time has brought changes. In 'St Germain, Val Clusone' (*Waldenses*, p. 67), the spindly looking bridge, which Dr Beattie pronounced 'picturesque,' was replaced by the present stone one shortly after Bartlett made his sketch. Pignerol, by day or night, is very different from Bartlett's sketch, but the view over it to the Cottian Alps remains the same and the Cathedral still stands, although not so openly as in the engraving (*Waldenses*, p. 20). The Protestant church that Bartlett visited at Bobbi Val Pelice has disappeared, and the mountain stream now rushes along under the main street; otherwise the scene at Bobbi is little altered.

An interesting comparison can be made between the prints of 'St Germain, Val Clusone' and the one of 'Outlet of Lake Memphremagog' (*Canadian Scenery*, ii, 17), which Bartlett sketched three years later in the Eastern Townships of Quebec. Their similarity reveals how much Bartlett's interpretation of the Canadian scene was influenced by his European background. Broadly speaking the Canadian drawing has the same picturesque elements as the one in the Clusone valley: the prospect, the wooden bridge, the figures in the foreground, the rapids in the Magog river, the rocks, the twisted trees, and the church tower. Although Sugar Loaf and the hills beyond Lake Memphremagog tower up rather too impressively, they convey the same kind of sublimity as the peaks beyond St Germain.

What distinguishes the two pictures are the details which Bartlett was always so interested in putting in his sketches: the architecture of the church towers, the dress of the labouring people, the construction of the bridges, the animals shown, the openness of the Canadian village scene, and the barrenness of the

Italian view. Both pictures illustrate the artist's attention to topography, which makes it easy for today's traveller to orient his map so that its symbols correspond with the artist's landscape. Of course many of the architectural features of Bartlett sketches, especially those of Canada, have completely disappeared.

By the end of 1835 and during the winter of 1836, the artist was sketching in the Low Countries for Professor N.G. van Kampen's *History and Topography of Holland and Belgium*. The fifty-one Bartlett sketches are nearly all architectural for as Van Kampen explained in his Preface: 'Holland and Belgium produce few of the grand or sublime characteristics of nature, except when we trace the meanderings of the Meuse; but though the banks of the other numerous rivers which irrigate this fruitful land, seldom excite the admiration, with the wild romantic scenery of that mighty stream, the Rhine ... still is the lover of the picturesque charmed with the diversified character of the landscapes, which so enchantingly illustrate the rich luxuriance and fertility of pastoral and domestic scenery ... '[46]

For the *History and Topography of Holland and Belgium*, Bartlett made many delicate drawings of famous buildings: the town halls at the Hague, Ypres, Bruges, Ghent, Leyden, Audenarde, Brussels, and Delft; churches and cathedrals at Rotterdam, Utrecht, Antwerp, Malines, Brussels; of the Great Tower at Bruges, the Dom Tower at Utrecht, and the Tower of the Exchange in Bruges; of the Egg-Market, and the Fish Market in Antwerp.

Again it is interesting to put Bartlett's picture of the 'Market Place, Furnes' (*Holland and Belgium*, p. 167) alongside 'The Market Place, Quebec' (*Canadian Scenery*, II, 11). What is very noticeable is the artist's use of light and shade – not as William Gilpin used it to contrast large areas, but rather to highlight interesting architectural units: the typical Dutch façades of the left and right of the main buildings in Furnes, and the west front of the Roman Catholic Basilica in Quebec City. In both pictures he attempts to portray groups of people at their daily round in the market square, but as always they remain rather indistinct and unreal in contrast with the charming, carefully sketched buildings. Of the two pictures, the Quebec one is much the better both because of its design and because of the greater freedom of the drawing.

The original sketch of 'The Market Place, Quebec' reveals also how faithful the engraver, F.W. Topham, was to the original.[47] The only significant difference in the engraving is the insertion of an additional figure. This sketch and others held in the National Gallery of Canada and in the Art Gallery of Ontario were done with a fine brush using a wash. The effect is nearly that of pen and ink with here and there flake-white used to indicate areas of light. Perhaps this work was done some time after the artist had made his preliminary sketch, but it is equally possible that the sketch was completed on the spot. The cloud effects may have been left to the engraver's imagination, but in sketches like the 'Junction of the Ottawa and St Lawrence,' and the 'Long Sault Rapid,'[48] Bartlett does indicate clouds and the rays of the sun.

Bartlett seems to be better known for his sketches for the two books *American Scenery* and *Canadian Scenery* than for anything else he did. Certainly those works fetch the highest prices today and are now much sought-after collector's items. The sketches for both volumes were done during three visits to America in 1836–7, 1838, and 1841. All the plates in *American Scenery* bear the dates 1837, 1838, 1839, and those in *Canadian Scenery* 1840, 1841, and 1842. In *American Scenery* the plates are arranged chronologically; in *Canadian Scenery* the arrangement is rather haphazard and according to region. As so often happened with Virtue's illustrated travel books, *Canadian Scenery* and *American Scenery*, like *Switzerland Illustrated*, appeared first in separate numbers containing a few engravings and available to the public for as little as two shillings and sixpence a number. On 30 March 1839 *Chamber's Edinburgh Journal* noted that *American Scenery* was then 'in the course of publication, twenty out of thirty parts having already appeared.' Each part contained four views 'with appropriate letterpress.'

Beattie says that on his first visit to America Bartlett spent nearly a year in the country (July or August 1836 – July 1837); the second tour in 1838 lasted from early summer to December and was mostly spent in Canada; the 1841 trip (March–December) was 'an extensive tour of the Northern and Southern States.' The 1842 date on seventeen of the engravings of the Maritimes in *Canadian Scenery* may indicate that these scenes were done on the third visit. The assumption here, of course, is that the dates on the engravings bear some relation to the time the sketch was made, but this may well be wrong because three other plates in *Canadian Scenery* bear the date 1842: 'Orford Mountain' (II, 15), 'Three Rivers' (I, 117), and, rather out of place, 'Navy Island' (I, 90). Finally, three plates of the Maritimes, 'Indian Town, River St. John' (II, 105), 'St. John from the Signal' (II, 106), and 'St. John and Portland' (II, 106) all have the date 1841.

Lacking his letters or journals of this period, it is only possible to guess at Bartlett's travel schedule in America. The maps in *American Scenery* and in *Canadian Scenery* do, however, show the routes and the places, with the exception of Lac des Allumettes, where 'views' were taken. Certainly, there was nothing remarkably original about the selection of the routes or places. Most of his views were of well-known sites. Tourist or traveller's guides were plentiful. In 1834 Harper and Brothers of New York brought out the third edition of *The Tourist; or Pocket Manual for Travellers on the Hudson River, the Western Canal and Stage Road to Niagara Falls down Lake Ontario and the St Lawrence to Montreal and Quebec comprising also the Routes to Lebanon, Ballston and Saratoga Springs*. Had Bartlett consulted it, he would have found, as its Preface asserts, that it was 'emphatically the pocket-companion of the traveller.' He would have been pleased to know that the Hudson was 'a noble river, abounding with scenery of the most sublime, picturesque and romantic character; not surpassed, for variety and grandeur, by any in the world.' He would have been reminded that he should take time on his way up the Hudson to view the Catterskill Fall which must be seen, as in his sketch, 'from below to produce the best effect.'

By consulting such a pocket manual Bartlett would know that the Mohawk and Hudson railroad had replaced the packet boat between Albany and Schenectady, and that from Schenectady west the traveller used the canal packet boat to Rochester, where a railroad linked that city with the steamboat landing on the Genesee River. 'Passengers will find this,' announces the *Manual*, 'a convenient place of embarcation for York, u.c., Niagara Falls, and all the other ports on Lake Ontario and the St Lawrence River.' A little later the *Manual* explains that some travellers prefer to take the Oswego canal from Syracuse to Oswego and 'then proceed by steamboat on Lake Ontario to Lewiston, whence a stage ride of seven miles takes them to the Falls.' Bartlett's route indicates that he did take this alternative.

The *Manual* would have helped him on his Canadian tour. It would give him eight pages of detail about Niagara Falls, 'the grandest spectacle in the world,' 'a majestic river,' 'truly sublime,' and would even quote Hennepin's description of the 'vast and prodigious Cadence of Water, which falls down after a surprising and astonishing manner, insomuch that the Universe does not afford its Parallel.'[49] The *Manual* would draw attention to the 'splendid view' from Terrapin Bridge, which Bartlett sketched showing the tower and the extension 'over the precipice of the Crescent Falls' (*American Scenery*, I, 32). This detailed description would supplement the accounts of Niagara which Bartlett knew from other sources such as Chateaubriand's *Atala* (1801) to which he refers in his letter of 23 October 1836 (B119).

From the information in the *Pocket Manual for Travellers*, the artist could find out much about Upper and Lower Canada. He could make his way to Sir Isaac Brock's first monument which he sketched before it was blown up by one of the 1837 rebels in 1840, learn of the times of departure of the steamboats from Lewiston, ascertain that York was 'a busy, bustling town,' and that the Rideau Canal had been in operation only a short time. At Prescott Bartlett would find 'two fine steamboats ... constructed especially with a view to running the rapids.' At Dickinson's Landing he would have to take a stagecoach for twelve miles to avoid the Long Sault, where he stopped to sketch the canal being built. After the Long Sault he could embark again for Coteau du Lac passing on his way St Regis, where he made his drawing of the Indian village. Montreal was now at hand, and the *Manual* vaguely indicated that tourists should also see Quebec for it had 'many attractions for strangers, grand fortifications, and beautiful scenery.'

The Canadian scene from Quebec City to Niagara had, like the Hudson, been described many times. Two examples may suffice. In 1807 George Heriot, the deputy postmaster-general of British North America, published his *Travels through the Canadas containing a Description of the Picturesque Scenery on Some of the Rivers and Lakes*. This work was 'illustrated with a map and numerous engravings from drawings made at several places by the author.' The well-known engravings of the 'Falls of Montmorenci,' 'Jeune Lorette,' and 'Falls of the Grande Chaudière' appear in this volume. 'The falls of Niagara,' remarks Heriot, 'surpass in sublimity every description which the powers of language can afford of that celebrated scene, the most wonderful and awful which the habitable world presents.'[50] Like Niagara, the Falls of Montmorenci also 'produce an effect awfully grand, and wonderfully sublime.'[51]

In 1815 Joseph Bouchette, the surveyor-general of Lower Canada, published *A Topographical Description of the Province of Lower Canada with Remarks upon Upper Canada*. His volume was 'embellished by several views, plans of harbors, battles, etc.' Bouchette's name, like those of Heriot, James Pattison Cockburn, Robert A. Sproule, and George Bourne, is often linked with Bartlett's, and it is perhaps too often asserted that Bartlett referred to their work when he was finishing his own sketches. A careful study of Bouchette's or of Cockburn's print of Fort Chambly, for example, of R.A. Sproule's 'Notre Dame Street, Montreal,' or of Thomas Davies' 'View of Montmorenci Falls,' in relation to Bartlett's sketches of the same scenes raises doubt about Bartlett's indebtedness to the earlier artists. Bartlett had no need to rely upon the work of these men because he was already a very competent topographical artist before he ever came to America. His Canadian sketches reveal that his technique and style did not change to suit prevailing tastes or examples here.

Not willing or able to take the time to leave the more frequented routes, Bartlett usually sketched the picturesque or sublime views that were reasonably close and often identifiable because other travellers and artists had referred to them. Working as he did on commission from Virtue, having no 'permanent share or copyright' of his works, being often absent from home for long periods, it was really little wonder that he kept to fairly well-known itineraries, which would give him the best chance to fill his portfolio with sketches for the machine of which he was so important a part.

Particularly in the United States he was also able to get advice and help from the well-known American author, journalist, and traveller, Nathaniel Parker Willis. Willis had travelled extensively in the Eastern United States and in 1827 and 1836 had visited Niagara Falls by way of the Erie Canal; on his 1827 trip he had continued on to Montreal. Willis' biographer, Henry A. Beers, says that Willis travelled about with Bartlett in 1837 and at that time decided to build his home, 'Glenmary,' near the junction of the Susquehanna River and the Owaga Creek. Willis, in fact, writes one of the few contemporary accounts of Bartlett, who visited him at Glenmary in the autumn of 1838:

Bartlett has been here a week ... We have climbed every hill-top that has the happiness of looking down on the Owaga and Susquehannah, and he agrees with me that a more lovely and habitable valley has never sat to him for its picture ... He has enriched his portfolio with four or five delicious sketches ...

How long since was it that I wrote to you of Bartlett's visit to Constantinople? Not more than four or five weeks, it seems to me; and yet here he is, on his return from a professional trip to *Canada*, with all its best scenery snug in his portmanteau! He steamed to Turkey and back, and steamed again to America, and will be once more in England in some twenty days – having visited and sketched the two extremities of the civilized world ... It seemed odd to me to turn over a drawing-book, and find on one leaf a freshly pencilled sketch of a mosque, and on the next a view of Glenmary – my turnip-field in the foreground. And then the man himself – pulling a Turkish para and a Yankee shin-plaster from his pocket with the same pinch – shuffling to breakfast in my *abri* on the Susquehannah, in a pair of peaked slippers of Constantinople, that smell as freshly of the bazaar as if they were bought yesterday – waking up with

41

'*pekke*! *pekke*! my good fellow!' when William brings him his boots – and never seeing a blood-red maple (just turned with the frost), without fancying it the sanguine flag of the Bosphorus or the bright red jacket of a Greek!⁵²

Willis concludes his account by describing how he and Bartlett burned log-heaps and remarks that the sight 'edifies the traveller who has bought wood by the pound in Paris, or stiffened for the want of it in the disforested Orient, to stand off a rifle-shot from a crackling wood, and toast himself by a thousand cords burnt for the riddance.' The sight of the flames reminded Willis of forest fires he had seen and he comments: 'We want an American Tempesta or "Savage Rosa" to "wreak" such pictures on canvas; and perhaps the first step to it would be the painting of the foliage of an American Autumn.'

Willis' account makes clear that Bartlett's preliminary sketches were done in pencil, and that even such a seasoned traveller as Willis was astonished at Bartlett's itinerary. Having returned from the Middle East in March 1838, Bartlett had sailed directly to Canada – perhaps Quebec – had travelled westward to Niagara and then apparently had gone by way of the Erie Canal to Lyons and south to Owaga, where he visited with Willis for a week before taking the New York and Erie Railroad to New York and sailing for England in December.

Beattie says that Bartlett, on his way back from the Middle East in 1838, 'touched at the more celebrated islands of the Archipelago' (B123) and spent some time sketching in Sicily. Apparently Virtue had encouraged Bartlett to bring out a book on Sicily, for in a letter dated 10 May 1840 Bartlett assured Beattie that Virtue was willing to undertake a work on Sicily 'though not immediately.' This book did not appear until 1853. It may have been on this trip in 1838 that Bartlett made some of the illustrations which appeared in George N. Wright's *The Shores and Islands of the Mediterranean*, [1840], and *The Rhine, Italy, and Greece*, 1841.

Just three of the illustrations in *The Shores and Islands of the Mediterranean* bear Bartlett's name: 'Town and Harbour of Salerno' (p. 145), 'Naples, from the Villa Falconnet' (p. 149), and 'Napoli di Romania, the Ancient Nauplia' (p. 152). Four other illustrations of Valetta and Corfu are the work of Samuel Prout based upon drawings 'from nature by Lieut. H.E. Allen, Rˡ Engʳ.' The original sketch of 'Town and Harbour of Salerno' is a good example of Bartlett's work: the exaggerated peaks behind the town, the attention given to prominent buildings, the interest in a landscape with valleys leading off into the distance, the effective use of light and shade, the rough foreground with the stunted, twisted trees and cactus, and finally the artist's use of flake-white to highlight figures, sails on boats, and, rather curiously, the branches of one of the trees in the left foreground. The engraving is faithful to the original in every respect but that of light and shade. In particular it fails to give the impression of the haze of heat which lies over the landscape in the original.

Of the engravings in *The Rhine, Italy, and Greece*, twenty-two are based upon Bartlett sketches. Eight are of scenes on the Rhine, thirteen belong to Italy, and one is of Mistra in Greece. The Italian ones indicate that Bartlett at one time travelled extensively in Italy; it is difficult to believe that he had time to do so on his way home in 1838. The engravings show scenes of Florence, Ancona, Sorrento, Genoa, Tivoli, Verona, the Bay of Baiae, Milan, Rome, and Pisa. The Rhine scenes, with the exception of the 'Island of Nonnenwerth,' lie between Coblentz and Bingen and include Stolzenfels, Ems, Braubach, and Rheinfels. It is just possible, of course, that all the Rhine sketches may date back to 1831 when 'Bartlett made an excursion of ten days up the Rhine, the first and happiest of that long series of travels with which his name is so honourably identified' (B105). The fact that he exhibited in the Royal Academy in 1833 two landscape pictures, 'Castle of Lahneck nr. Coblentz' and 'Castle of Rheinfels,' is further evidence that the Rhine sketches may belong to this 1831 excursion. Generally the Italian scenes are more effective than those on the Rhine, in which the background is so often made up of indistinct hill masses. A comparison of the background of 'Bingen, on the Rhine' (II, 25) with that in the 'Arch of Trajan, Ancona' (I, 70) reveals at once how much more interesting the architectural features of Ancona are than the fuzzy hill slopes of the Rhine.

In his *Brief Memoir*, Beattie refers at length to the seven months (15 August 1837 – March 1838) that Bartlett spent preparing the sketches for the 83 steel engravings which appear in Julia Pardoe's *The Beauties of the Bosphorus*, which was published in 1839.[53] In a letter to Beattie from Pera, October 1837, Bartlett describes Constantinople and the surrounding country in fine weather as ' ... a vast phantasmagoria – very much like a moving diorama full of scenes from fairy tales ... impossible for the pencil to express its beauties as they are scattered about in a manner very puzzling to the artist. And how express the oriental light – which without the accidents of light and shade usual in the north – is sufficient to produce the most brilliant relief combined with a softness and

43

harmony equally beautiful. I fear we can only give the mere form of the objects viewed – but not that beautiful lustre with which in the East they are always invested.' In the same letter Bartlett says that he is reading Gibbon as he moves about and tries to imagine past events in Constantinople. He cannot decide upon sending home drawings to Virtue as he has not heard from him. If the weather holds he hopes he can spend a month in Asia. Pera, where he is staying, is 'a miserable hole.' There is a word of caution about Miss Pardoe and a puzzling reference to a projected work that he and Beattie are planning – possibly one on the scenery of the Danube.

These were years when Bartlett's popularity was high. Attractive travel books containing engravings of his sketches sold remarkably well at home and abroad. Reviewers praised his work as Virtue published volume after volume, the illustrations of which – varied and picturesque – reminded readers of places as far apart as the Golden Horn and the Catterskill Falls.

IV

No wonder Willis in Glenmary was struck by the contrast of the drawings in Bartlett's portfolio. How compare 'A Scene in the Tchartchi' (*Beauties of the Bosphorus*, p. 32) with the sketch of the 'Fish-Market, Toronto' (*Canadian Scenery*, I, 88); 'The Bosphorus from above the Beshik-Tash' (*Beauties of the Bosphorus*, p. 19) with the view of 'Halifax, from Dartmouth' (*Canadian Scenery*, II, 115); or 'A Turkish Apartment in the Fanar' (*Beauties of the Bosphorus*, p. 125) with 'A Shanty on Lake Chaudière' (*Canadian Scenery*, II, 64)? What was common to all the drawings, however, was their fidelity to the original scene. John Carne speaks of 'the artist who has so faithfully and admirably sketched the various views of this mountain and the rest of Syria.'[54] Julia Pardoe, back in England from her expedition to Turkey, gazes 'on the extraordinarily faithful and admirable sketches which lie upon [her] table ... from the pencil of Mr. Bartlett' and considers that her 'hour of real enjoyment has arrived.'[55]

One of the major reasons for the popularity of Bartlett's American and Canadian scenes today is that the tourist or amateur collector of prints can nearly always associate a Bartlett view with the former landscape of his country or even the landscape today. Writing about two prints in *Canadian Scenery*, 'The Burial Place of the Voyageurs' and 'Working a Canoe up a Rapid,' Eric Morse comments that, although 'Neither the canoes nor the men's hats are at all accurately depicted ... the terrain in both cases is portrayed so well that the two spots are almost certainly recognizable as being, respectively, the Des Chats Portage looking down the Ottawa, and the lower end of the Portage Dufort (now obliterated by Hydro).'[56]

Bartlett engravings of scenes in the Middle East generally lack the kind of roughness which Gilpin demanded in the picturesque and emphasize romantic qualities of strangeness and beauty in ancient cities: Turkish shipping in the port of Constantinople, graceful minarets above the mosque of Eyoub, cypresses in moonlight on the 'Petit Champ-des-Morts' at Pera. This is not to say that the travellers to the East were uninterested in roughness and wildness. In commenting upon Lady Hester Stanhope's villa, John Carne describes the scene as one 'which Mrs Radcliffe would have selected for a romance, but ... it wants the gloom of the dark forests, the exquisite solitudes that stir the soul.'[57] Even the scenery in the mountains of Lebanon is inferior 'in many points to that of the Alps.'[58] But if 'savage Rosa' could not be so often evoked, the East did stir the travellers in other ways. For Bartlett, 'Every object [was] novel and Oriental in character, and independent of its picturesque beauty, [was] linked by a delicious association with our earliest dreams of Biblical scenery and incident.'[59]

It is undoubtedly the associations of the East with biblical history which account nearly always for Bartlett's interest in the land. At vesper time in the Church of the Sepulchre in Jerusalem his emotions are deeply stirred by its 'venerable antiquity and gorgeous gloom.' The sight calls to his mind 'the long series of pilgrims, monks, and warriors, who during so many centuries had worshipped around the Sacred Tomb.'[60]

Nothing struck him in America, remarked Bartlett, 'so much as its comparative want of *associations*.'[61] Here he had to accept a landscape nearly empty of architecture, of all the monuments that keep tradition alive. In Canada, with exceptions like the Basilica in Quebec and the Cathedral in Montreal, the buildings he sketched such as the residence of Judge Haliburton, the Governor's House in Fredericton, or Ontario House in Toronto, could hardly have appealed to him as much as the picturesque log shanties and Indian tepees which he so often included in his sketches.

In the United States, however, he could find attractive street scenes and buildings, which may have reminded him a little of those he did for Thomas Wright's *Essex*. Some obviously delighted him: Faneuil Hall in Boston, the

45

Park and City Hall of New York, the main street of Utica, Ballston Springs, and Yale College at New Haven. He also discovered picturesque vistas at Albany, Fort Putnam, Hyde Park, Newburgh, New York Bay, Peekskill Landing, and Harper's Ferry, which were really very like some of those he had seen and drawn in Europe.

But if America lacked tradition and associations, it offered the artist some compensation. Almost as if he were answering Bartlett's criticism, Willis argued in his Introduction to *American Scenery* that 'the picturesque views of the United States suggest a train of thought directly opposite to that of similar objects of interest in other lands' where 'the soul and centre of attraction in every picture is some ruin of the *past*.' He who travels in America, says Willis, rather grandly, 'must feed his imagination on the *future*.' 'Instead of looking through a valley, which has presented the same aspect for hundreds of years ... [the American] sees a valley laden down like a harvest waggon ... and his first thought is of the villages that will soon sparkle on the hill-sides, the axes that will ring from the woodlands, and the mills, bridges, canals, and railroads, that will span and border the stream ... ' Willis also argues that the richest source of the picturesque in America lies in its river scenery, and he even defends 'the general architecture' saying that 'many of the public buildings especially are, as works of art, well worthy the draughtsman's notice.'

Whether Bartlett took his friend's advice or whether he merely recorded what he saw is not known. But that he was much taken by the 'march of mind' in America is obvious in his sketches of canals, railroad scenes, bridges, steamships, barges, ferries, viaducts, fertile river valleys, mills, waterworks, and municipal buildings. The full consequence of this industrial progress, however, was not at all obvious in 1837–8. Too frequently a Bartlett print now calls to mind what man has done to spoil or deface his inheritance; along many American and Canadian rivers it is today sometimes difficult to reconstruct the picturesque views that charmed artists early in the nineteenth century.

Both *Canadian Scenery* and *American Scenery* display Bartlett's interest in forms of transportation in the new world. In the towns and cities of the United States both horses and oxen appear on the streets. There is a wide variety of conveyances: carriages, wagons, democrats, two-wheeled carts, and horse-drawn city buses. Canoes appear ten times as frequently on Canadian waterways as on those of the United States, but canal barges appear only in the States where canal systems like the Erie had ensured the supremacy of the Hudson–

New York trade route over the St Lawrence–Quebec route. The Bartlett print, 'Village of Little Falls' (*American Scenery*, II, 40), showing both canal and rail traffic is one such indication of American enterprise. In Canada, however, transportation systems were just being developed. One of the prints in *Canadian Scenery* shows the excavation of the Long Sault Canal and another the shining locks of the newly built Rideau Canal. Bartlett probably used Canada's first railroad to complete his journey to Montreal in 1838, after he crossed from Georgeville by way of the Bolton Pass to St Jean on the Richelieu River.

Of all the activities on water which took Bartlett's attention in Canada, none seems to have interested him more than the rafting operations of the timber trade: the great 'drams' pitching down wild reaches of rapids on the St Lawrence, weathering storms on Lake St Peter, and gathering quietly at Cap Santé before massing finally in the Quebec timber depots; the smaller rafts, complete with a tepee-like shelter, small fire, and mast, drifting through quiet water at Brockville or, with all hands straining to direct them, entering the rapids on the approach to the village of Cedars. On the Ottawa River Bartlett left a visual record of the timber slides that enabled the rafts to pass the rapids on the way down the St Lawrence. It was an interesting picturesque activity that belonged to the Canadian wilderness and provided an exciting substitute for civilized landscapes rich in tradition and monumental buildings.

Although the Canadian landscape was strikingly different from that of Switzerland, Bartlett's approach to it in terms of composition was much the same as that he used, for example, in *Switzerland Illustrated*, where he so often sought out a point of view which would offer him a 'prospect.' Nearly half of the sketches in *Canadian Scenery* were made from a hillside, and many of the remainder were from rivers or lakes where the artist's vision was unrestricted. The Canadian scenes, more than the American ones, suffered because so often the background had to be the unrelieved, dull mantle of unending forests, which may explain Bartlett's willingness in the Eastern Townships to suggest a decidedly mountainous terrain. By sketching from the base of hills and waterfalls, he often succeeded in creating the kind of picture that may have stirred some emotion of horror, some astonishment in the minds of his public. The best examples in *Canadian Scenery* are the towering, broken crags that loom up from the stormy Bay of Fundy (II, 114); the Jungfrau-like mountain that takes up the background of 'A Lake Farm on the Frontier' (II, 26); the Gibraltar-like heights of the 'Citadel of Kingston' (I, 62); the mass of Belœil Mountain at

Fort Chambly on the Richelieu (1, 84); and the mountain at Montreal as seen from the St Lawrence (1, 114).[62]

As in Switzerland he found some of his best picturesque views by standing at the edge of precipices or gorges or by waterfalls and sketching the whirlpool at Niagara, the Montmorency Fall, Les Marches Naturelles near Quebec, the Chaudière at Bytown, the village of Lorette, the Portage des Chats, and Split Rock on the St John River.

What does happen, however, in both the American and Canadian views is that more emphasis is placed upon the foreground and middleground to compensate for the lack of variety in the forest-shrouded backgrounds. Rosa's and Gilpin's blasted trees, angular rocks, and forest scenes are nearly always present in the foreground, where the conventional groups of people gave Bartlett a chance to describe the life of the people – labourers, tradesmen, and military – at work: raftsmen holding their drams on course, voyageurs portaging, Indians selling fish and making birch bark canoes, farmers taking in their crops, the military off-duty at Bytown and Kingston, labourers building a broad esplanade at Quebec, fishermen bringing in a net at Wellington on Lake Ontario, pioneers making a clearing in the wilderness, drovers ferrying cattle at Georgeville, men at work at a sawmill, and lobster fishermen at their boats in Annapolis.

It is Bartlett's fidelity to the contemporary scene in 1838 and 1841 which accounts for the appearance of so many of his prints in popular history books, such as Edwin C. Guillet's *Pioneer Travel in Upper Canada* and T.R. Glover and D.D. Calvin's *A Corner of Empire*. In an introductory comment upon the five Bartlett engravings in their book, Glover and Calvin refer only to 'one or two minor inaccuracies' in the pictures in *Canadian Scenery*. It is interesting, for example, to compare Calvin's photographs of timber rafting on the St Lawrence with the Bartlett prints that were sketched fifty years earlier and to note the accuracy of the artist's pencil. 'March on Lake Chaudière' (1, 80) not only discloses how rafting on the Ottawa differed from that on the St Lawrence but also shows the beginning of settlement in the wilderness where a wharf, post office, and church have been built. Other than the cloud effects the content of the print is exactly the same as the original sketch.[63]

One art critic, Gérard Morisset, in his *Peintures et tableaux* (1936), has questioned the topographical accuracy of some of the Bartlett views and should, for this reason, be heard: 'Si Bartlett dessine habituellement avec précision, il lui arrive souvent de négliger l'exactitude parfait des détails. L'ensemble de ses dessins est juste, sans doute; certaines parties architecturales le sont beaucoup moins. Ainsi une gravure du *Canada Pittoresque* fait voir *le Cap-Santé vu du Saint-Laurent*. [1, 121] Au premier plan, des radeaux à voiles et des barques; au fond, le village perché entre les deux falaises. Regardez l'église: c'est une caricature de l'édifice construit de 1755 à 1763, caricature d'autant plus incontestable que cette église n'a pas subi de modifications importantes depuis 1822.'

Morisset maintains that he could 'multiplier les exemples de telles inexactitudes,' which serve to diminish Bartlett's reputation as a 'parfait dessinateur.' Unfortunately Morisset weakens his argument by referring to oils of Montreal which are now generally accepted as forgeries just as some of Victor De Grailly's oils of the Hudson River are now known to be copies based upon Bartlett illustrations. Morisset's references to bibliographical detail is confused and, on occasion, inaccurate. His conclusion is too general, too authoritative, even a little arrogant: 'Bartlett est un topographe. C'est tout. Il n'est féru ni d'originalité, ni d'harmonie. Chargé de faire connaître le Nouveau monde aux bourgeois moyens de Londres, il recherche plus la vraisemblance que la vérité absolue; plus le chic de l'exécution que l'effet vraiment artistique. Parfois il attrape le pittoresque, il soulève un coin de poésie.' It is impossible, says Morisset, to compare Bartlett to Dreux, Devéria, and Lami – French artists who are now little known or praised. When Morisset compares Bartlett's work unfavourably with that of the early Corot, we can grant the justness of his criticism, but later in the same paragraph we may not accept his assumption that: 'Même au Canada, Bartlett supporte mal le parallèle avec Georges Hériot, avec les Bouchette père et fils, avec Richard Dillon, Cockburn et James Duncan.'[64]

Little need be said about Nathaniel Parker Willis' contribution to the 'Literary Department' of *American Scenery, Canadian Scenery*, or for that matter, *The Scenery and Antiquities of Ireland*. Willis was, as Edgar Allan Poe pointed out, 'a graceful trifler,' who never hesitated to quote at length from other authors who deserved, as he put it, 'to be better known.' Henry A. Beers notes that Willis' 'three books on American, Canadian, and Irish scenery were hack work' and that there was 'little of personal or purely literary interest in them ... *Canadian Scenery* was "lifted" almost entire, from the narratives of Charlevoix, Adair, Heriot, Hodgson, Murray, Talbot, Cockburn, and other travelers and historians'[65] and not always, as Beers maintains, 'with ample acknowledgements.'

But the lack of Willis' own work did not detract at all from the quality of many of the authors he chose to quote from. The Englishman at home would find

49

Edward Allen Talbot's account of a bear hunt in the wilds of western Ontario much more to his taste than Willis' own account of his life among the British aristocracy, which so annoyed the influential *Quarterly Review* in 1835. Likewise, the Englishman would approve of the account written by 'the wife of an emigrant officer' of pioneer life in the Peterborough area. 'From her admirable, graphic, and womanly records,' admits Willis, 'we make large extracts.' Some eighteen thousand words from Catharine Parr Traill's *The Backwoods of Canada* follow this admission (*Canadian Scenery*, II, 58–92). The overall effect, however, of such quotations is to strengthen the realistic quality of the Bartlett sketches of pioneer life. Mrs Traill saw pioneer life very much as it was and, although 'sugar-boilers, with their bright logfire among the trees,' made 'a pretty and picturesque sight,' she made clear to her English readers that there was 'a want of picturesque beauty' and of 'venerable antiquity in the Canadian woods.'[66] It is interesting to note in this connection that, when Bartlett was editor of *Sharpe's London Journal* in 1849, he placed the engraving of his sketch, 'A Shanty on Lake Chaudière,' opposite Mrs Traill's story, 'The Settlers Settled; or Pat Connor and his Two Masters.'

Despite Mrs Traill's first-hand accounts of pioneer settlements and Bartlett's sketches of log shanties in forest clearings, the wilderness remained attractively picturesque for many Englishmen living at home in the warm radiance of the Romantic movement. This much George Virtue certainly realized for he had his fingers firmly on the pulse of a large segment of the well-to-do Victorian public. It was a strong pulse that responded generously to the handsome volumes from his press on American and Canadian scenery 'illustrated in a series of views' by that indefatigable traveller and artist, William Henry Bartlett.

v

From 1836 to 1841, Bartlett was engaged for varying periods preparing illustrations for the two-volume sets of William Beattie's *Scotland Illustrated* (1838) and N.P. Willis' *The Scenery and Antiquities of Ireland* (1842). Of the seventeen Bartlett prints in volume I of *Scotland Illustrated* all but one bear the date 1837, which indicates that they may have been sketched in the spring of 1836. Only two Bartletts appear in volume II, and these were taken from pictures by other artists. According to Willis, all of the 120 engravings for the volumes on Ireland were taken from original Bartlett sketches done during the second half of 1839. Other engravings of Scottish scenes of this period may be found in Allan Cunningham's *The Poems, Letters, and Land of Robert Burns* (1840), which contains thirty-three Bartletts, four of which also appear in *Scotland Illustrated*. The Cunningham illustrations all belong to the Burns country; in some of them the unattractive life of the people in cold, grimy villages and towns crowds out the picturesque. To this group belong 'Poosie Nansie's House, Mauchline' (I, v), 'The Market Place, Dumfries' (I, xxxviii), 'Leith Pier and Harbour' (I, 158), 'The House in which Burns Died, Dumfries' (II, 394), and 'Globe Close, Dumfries' (II, 85). Two engravings in these volumes are, however, as pleasing as any Bartletts that belong to this period: 'Ayr Water at Staer' (II, 246) with its classical prospect; and 'The Twa Brigs, Ayr' (II, 178), bridges that complement each other well and afford glimpses of the town beyond with its soaring spire.

In Scotland and in Ireland Bartlett could select, as Willis said, 'his point of view so as to bring prominently into his sketch, the castle or the cathedral, which history or antiquity [had] hallowed.' The picturesque artist, furthermore, could also find for 'every picture ... some ruin of the *past*.'[67] Willis very well knew that Bartlett's real interests lay a long way off from the turnip fields of Glenmary. In sketch after sketch of Scottish and Irish scenery Bartlett demonstrated his romantic love for 'old, unhappy far-off things': roofless Alloway Kirk, the ruins of Corsregal Castle and Lincluden College, desecrated Jedburgh Abbey, Dunseverich Castle, Dunluce Castle, the Abbeys of Sligo, Roserk, and Clare, and the seven churches of Clonmacnoise and of Glendalough.

To note the advance in Bartlett's artistic ability by 1839 as compared with a decade earlier, it is helpful to place such illustrations as 'The Four Courts, Dublin,' 'Glengariffe,' or 'The Upper Lake of Killarney,' as these appear in G.N. Wright's *Ireland Illustrated*, alongside their counterparts in N.P. Willis' *The Scenery and Antiquities of Ireland*. The most noticeable advance is the way in which Bartlett has learned to use light and shade to liven his picture. Buildings now have charm and seem more a part of the landscape than formerly. There is, in short, a more sensitive approach to the subject; the dry architectural drawing of 'The Four Courts' in 1829, for example, has been replaced by an aesthetically pleasing picture of the same scene in 1839 (*Scenery and Antiquities of Ireland*, II, 149).

Freed from the forest landscapes of America, Bartlett was able in his sketches

51

of Scotland and Ireland to deepen his backgrounds and emphasize the distant view that belongs to such delightful sketches as 'The Town of Dumfries' in *Scotland Illustrated* (I, 192); and to 'Waterford' (II, 91), 'Dublin Bay' (II, 161), 'Ballina' (I, 65), 'The Eagle Mountain, Killeries' (I, 81), and 'The Shannon' (I, 106) in *The Scenery and Antiquities of Ireland*. The interest of the Scottish and Irish engravings derives as much from the quality of the architectural drawing as it does from the representation of landscape. We are compelled to look upon the arching bridges of Ayr, the turrets and roof decoration of the castle of May-bole, the village houses and churches of Ballina, the mediaeval towers of Limerick and Waterford, and the traces of Spanish influence on buildings in Galway. Indeed, today, we are much more interested in the architectural details of the buildings and bridges in these prints than we are in the prospects which so delighted men like Beattie, whose reference to the Pass of Inverfarrakaig in Scotland illustrates so well what many Victorians looked for in their illustrated travel books. The Pass, says Beattie, is ' ... a defile which, in many respects, may vie with some of the minor passes of the Swiss Alps. It has all the characteristics usually observed in that country, glaciers excepted; and presents a combination of features rising in striking graduation, from the softness of cultivated landscape through the different stages of the beautiful, the picturesque, and romantic, till it closes the picture with those sublime and stupendous bulwarks with which Nature appears to exclude the habitable world.'[68] It was tastes such as this that account for the popularity of the picturesque as late as the 1850s and for the willingness of Virtue to commission Bartlett to provide sketches for three other works that appeared under Beattie's name: *The Ports, Harbours, Watering-Places, and Coast Scenery of Great Britain* [1842],[69] *The Danube* (1844), and *The Castles and Abbeys of England* (1844).

Beattie took over *The Ports, Harbours, and Watering-Places* from Edward and William Finden, who had been unable to pay for the expenses of the production; the letterpress descriptions of the second volume and the appendix of volume I are Beattie's, and the illustrations (fifteen in volume I, fifty-eight in volume II) are Bartlett's. These prints, with two or three exceptions, bear the dates 1840 or 1841. *The Ports, Harbours, and Watering-Places* was a handsome work, which observed the same conventions as the *Picturesque Views of the Southern Coast of England* (1826) for which J.M.W. Turner had made the drawings. A few of the Bartlett views can be compared favourably with Turner's; certainly 'New

Bridge and Bromielaw, Glasgow' (ii, 46), 'Conway Quay' (ii, 70), 'Redcliffe Church and Basin, Bristol' (ii, 107), 'Canning Dock and Custom House, Liverpool' (ii, 110), and 'General View of London' (i, 163) are representative of Bartlett's finest work.

In an undated letter (probably early in 1842) to Beattie, Bartlett describes his plans for his trip down the Danube to get material for Beattie's new book:

> I have obtained the *Handbook to Southern Germany* which notices most of the subjects of any consequence down the Danube from Ulm to the Black Sea.
>
> I see the most interesting part of the river is decidedly below Passau. I think of proceeding at once to Ratisbon – and thence descending perhaps to Buda, but possibly not below Vienna. I cannot leave for a few days, as there is some doubt about the boats running up the Rhine.
>
> As Virtue wishes me to select some subjects for cuts could you favour me with a list of subjects and the sketches as they will stand in your description because those first wanted must be of course [put] in hand first.
>
> My present journey differs in one respect from any other I have hitherto undertaken i.e. that it is at Virtue's own cost – and not as formerly at my own – this will of course prevent me from doing anything else unless previously arranged with him.

The *Handbook* to which Bartlett refers was likely Murray's *Handbook for Southern Germany*, for Beattie indicates that he found it 'one of the most popular works of the day' and quotes from it to support his impressions of the Defile of Kazan, which the *Handbook* described as a 'colossal gorge' that possessed 'awful grandeur.' Bartlett's reference to his journey being 'at Virtue's own cost' is one of the early indications that the demand for such illustrated travel books may have been declining.

The Danube, like *Switzerland Illustrated*, was devoted to whatever was picturesque in that river's 'course of nearly eighteen hundred miles, through Swabia, Bavaria, Austria, Hungary, and the Turco-Russian provinces of Servia, Bulgaria, Moldavia, and Bessarabia.'[70] Bartlett contributed sketches for the eighty steel engravings and nearly the same number of woodcuts. This time, however, Beattie says that most of the illustrations were 'taken on the spot by M. Abresch – a German artist of well-known talent and reputation – and drawn by Mr Bartlett, who has also contributed various original views, interspersed throughout the work.' One other interesting feature of *The Danube* rests in Beattie's acknowledgement that his manuscript had 'in several instances, been enriched by the graphic notes of Mr Bartlett, taken during his recent voyage down the Danube.'[71] One of Beattie's footnotes indicates that he was, in fact, working from an 'MS Journal' kept by the artist.[72]

The quality of the steel engravings is consistently good, and they reveal much careful detail of the landscape and attention to the lives of the people along the course of the river. Several prints like 'The Approach to Passau from Linz' show rafting operations very similar to those that Bartlett recorded on the St Lawrence and Ottawa rivers. A comparison, for example, of a photograph of Linz with a Bartlett print of the same scene reveals how concerned the artist was that his drawings should be topographically correct.

Indeed, it is Bartlett's close attention to scenic detail that redeems the monotony of many of his sketches, a monotony which comes about because of the point of view which he has to take if he is to satisfy the taste for the picturesque. Even 'The Park and City Hall, New York' (*American Scenery*, I, 103) is not strikingly different in its composition from that of 'Vienna, from the Bastions' (*The Danube*, p. 159); in the same way 'Albany' (*American Scenery*, I, 22) resembles 'Belgrade' (*The Danube*, p. 200); the 'View near Anthony's Nose, Hudson Highlands' (*American Scenery*, II, 90) resembles the 'Scene near the Weltenburg' (*The Danube*, p. 36); and 'Ballyshannon' in Ireland (*Scenery and Antiquities of Ireland*, I, 60) is like the 'Castle of Spielberg' (*The Danube*, p. 96). It is true that the occupations of the people in the foreground often emphasize the diversity of the sketches in *The Danube*, but groups of people may be sketched in as a kind of 'filler' and contribute little to the Danube scene as in the open space before Ulm Cathedral (p. 8), or in the foregrounds of 'Straubing' (p. 67), 'Passau' (p. 72), 'The Castle of Neuhaus' (p. 84), 'Linz' (p. 87), or of 'St. Stephen's Church' (p. 140). Fortunately for W.H. Bartlett, his early training with its emphasis on architectural detail and landscape drawing ensured that the conventions of his day did not altogether stifle his talent.

Beattie's last illustrated work, *The Castles and Abbeys of England* (1842–51), used in its second volume steel engravings and woodcuts taken from Bartlett sketches of Chepstow Castle, Tintern Abbey, Raglan Castle, Llanthony Abbey, and the castles of Uske, Pembroke, Manorbeer, and Kidwelly. These prints are attractive vignettes of castle and abbey ruins with little or no attention given to landscape. Generally they are plain views that lack the interest that attaches, for example, to those of *Scotland Illustrated*; in this latter book, however, the publisher had to expend about forty thousand pounds, a cost which Beattie

5 Town and Harbour of Salerno *sepia wash*

6 Peterborough Cathedral, View of the Church from the N.E. *water colour*

7 Peterborough Cathedral, View of the Church from the N.E. *steel engraving*

8 Thaxted Church, Essex *sepia wash*

9 Thaxted Church, Essex *steel engraving*

10 The Market Place, Quebec *steel engraving*

11 Market Place, Furnes *steel engraving*

12 Ruins of the Episcopal Palace, Sion *water colour*

13 Ruins of the Episcopal Palace, Sion *steel engraving*

14 Outlet of Lake Memphremagog *steel engraving*

15 St. Germain, Val Clusone *steel engraving*

16 View of the City of Wells from the s.e. *steel engraving*

17 Conway Quai *steel engraving*

18 Lower Pool of Gihon, Jerusalem *steel engraving*

19 Entrance by the Jaffa Gate *sepia wash*

20 Nazareth Looking towards the Plain of Esdraelon *steel engraving*

remarks 'confined the circulation of picturesque antiquarian works to the opulent classes of society.' *The Castles and Abbeys* was a much cheaper work 'being illustrated by original views taken on the spot, and not amounting in general to more than a twentieth of the price at which its predecessors in the same field have been published.'[73] That Bartlett himself was concerned about the quality of the *Castles and Abbeys* is obvious from an undated letter he wrote to Beattie while he was visiting his brother, the Reverend Frederick A. Bartlett, at Warrington. Beattie was asked to forward Bartlett's own estimates for plates in 'a new style of art' to Virtue. Bartlett does not indicate what the new style was but asserts that it should be *'very effective.'* The cost for two plates, the size of those in *Switzerland Illustrated*, would be ten guineas, and for eight vignettes, forty guineas.

There is little question at this time that costs and perhaps a surfeit of illustrated travel books, especially on the Middle East, were forcing Virtue to curtail such publications. It was not, for example, until 1847 that Bartlett saw the publication of some of the sketches he had made in the Middle East in 1842 (B126). These appeared as eighty steel engravings in Henry Stebbing's *The Christian in Palestine, or Scenes of Sacred History*. The delay could not be attributed to any falling away of the artist's powers. *The Critic* lauded the illustrations: 'Mr Bartlett has a remarkable eye for the picturesque; all his views are taken from good points. He never fails to present us with a perfect picture, full of objects of interest, and conveying a better idea of the place than any sketcher whose works we have seen of late years. What an acquisition it will be to quarto editions of the Bible!' The Reverend Henry Stebbing in his Preface to *The Christian in Palestine* reminded his readers 'that the pictorial illustrations of this volume may be regarded as faithfully descriptive of the scenes which they represent. Mr Bartlett's reputation is too well established to render this praise necessary. He is an experienced and intelligent traveller, as well as an accomplished artist.' In notes to the author, Bartlett himself made comments[74] upon one of his sketches, 'Nazareth looking towards the Plain of Esdraelon' (p. 49), which reveal not only his interest in picturesque 'forms and costume' but also his own analysis of the view:

It is rarely the case that a locality satisfies the imagination, but in this instance there was nothing wanting. The spreading trees above me bent over towards the valley, almost touching the ground, and seeming as a frame to confine the picture. The little valley lay below, encircled by hills of moderate height, alternately green and rocky, beneath which, half hidden, the white buildings of Nazareth appear to nestle for shelter; on the left the hills drop quietly to the valley beautifully broken by groups of trees and rocky fragments ...

The survey of the formation of the district was of itself curious, reminding me of the models of Swiss scenery often met with. The shape of the sequestered vale of Nazareth, branching out of the great plain of Esdraelon, with its sheltering hills, the plain itself, with the direction of its mountain-boundaries, were distinctly made out. A singular contrast is presented by the narrow valley and extensive plain: the former green, well shaded by olive-groves, and having on the sides of its boundaries occasional groups of large carob-trees; while the distant plain is one level sheet of corn, unrelieved by a single object.

Viewed from this precipice, which would seem to be identical with that from which the enraged Nazarenes sought to cast Jesus, the modern town lies at our feet; and, as *may be seen in the view*, some of its buildings cluster picturesquely among the trees on the hill-slopes above ... The whole extent of the town is not shown in the engraving: to say the truth, the view from this point is too map-like, and wants grouping. To the left of the valley of Nazareth, and on the side of the mountain, a touch of light shows the position of Nain; the vast plain of Esdraelon is in the distance.[75]

But in spite of favourable reviews and Bartlett's experience and artistic ability, 'the badness of the times' seems to have compelled Virtue to set the sketches for *The Christian in Palestine* aside for a few years until 1847.

The market for illustrated books on European countries was similarly affected. Some time before the publication of Cunningham's *The Poems, Letters, and Land of Burns* [1840], Virtue had agreed to bring out an illustrated work on France. In an undated letter to Beattie, Bartlett hopes that 'we shall go on together in perfect harmony and I shall be very glad as soon as I clearly understand the plan – i.e. whether to divide the work into chapters on the Ancient provinces – or to make a "Voyage Pittoresque" on the plan I mentioned – if the latter – the sooner I lay down the exact route the better as whenever I go to Paris I can continue to take in a considerable district in my way.' That Virtue eventually changed his mind about this work may have been influenced by the publication of such books as Morellet's *Le Nivernois album historique et pittoresque* (1838), Louisa Stuart Costello's *A Pilgrimage to Auvergne from Picardy to Le Velay* (1842), or George N. Wright's *France Illustrated*, which Fisher and Son published in 1845–7.

VI

It was undoubtedly the poor demand for large illustrated volumes on travel that compelled Bartlett to consider other means of making his livelihood and of accepting the idea put forward by Beattie that he should use 'his pen as well as his pencil' (B125). The outcome was *Walks about the City and Environs of Jerusalem* (1844), the result of his third visit to the East, which he undertook in 1842 after the completion of his trip down the Danube. The book was dedicated to the Reverend F.A. Bartlett by 'his affectionate brother,' and its 'principal object' was to put before the student interested in biblical history 'a picture' of what was described. The illustrations were '*generally* faithful and correct, nothing being added for mere picturesque effect.'[76]

The second edition in 1845 omitted the long quotations, which had been 'objected to' in the first, but kept the illustrations which had been praised for 'the good selection and general accuracy.'[77] After an introductory chapter which described his route to Jerusalem and a chapter devoted to the history of Jerusalem based in large part upon the writings of the historian Josephus and the writings of Robinson and Catherwood, Bartlett simply entitled the remaining chapters, 'Walks I, II, and III,' as he attempted 'to give a clear, connected, and accurate view of the City.'

At its best the prose is interesting when the author is describing his own impressions; at its worst it is dull and tedious when he becomes too involved in the minutiæ of history and the archaeological theories of scholars like Catherwood. The best is often sustained because of links with illustrations like that of 'Mount Zion, Jerusalem from the Hill of Evil Counsel.' After noting the references in *Paradise Lost* and in the book of Jeremiah to the Valley of Himnon, Bartlett sees ' ... something in the scenery of this valley, and the hill above, its tombs hewn in the rock, long since tenantless; the gray gloom of its old fig and olive-trees starting from the fissures of the crags – the overhanging wall of Zion, desolate almost as in the time of her captivity, that forcibly recalls the wild and mournful grandeur of the prophetic writings.'[78] Although the syntax is troublesome, the description is that of the topographical artist who has learned to see what many fail to see and whose romantic imagination has a rich store of literature to feed upon.

Bartlett acknowledges his debt to Chateaubriand's *Itinéraire de Paris à*

Jerusalem (1811) and especially to Lamartine's *Voyage en Orient* (1835), which he had, according to Beattie, 'perused among the very scenes which inspired it' (B118). Like Lamartine, Bartlett catches his first sight of Jerusalem at dawn; his impressions are his own: 'There was nothing grand or striking in the vision – a line of dull walls, a group of massive towers, a few dark olives, rising from a dead and sterile plain, were all that met the eye; yet, enough that this was Jerusalem – the Holy City: her mournful aspect well suits with the train of recollections she awakens.'[79] For Lamartine it is a 'mystérieuse et éblouissante apparition.' Jerusalem 'se détachait en jaune sombre et net, sur le fond bleu du firmament et sur le fond noir du mont des Oliviers.'[80] Bartlett sees the Holy Land as a topographer and historian; Lamartine, as a poet and devout Catholic. Both men are, of course, taken by its picturesque scenery and sublime associations. Lamartine can think only of Poussin or Claude Lorrain as he looks over the Plain of Zabulon. Bartlett is more factual than the Frenchman, more concerned to make sure his readers are with him as

... we slowly climb the steep ascent of the Mount of Olives, by one of the paths worn in the rock ... gaining, as we advance, grand glimpses of the city, through a picturesque foreground of its ancient trees. From the extreme summit the view is perhaps the most interesting in the world. Jerusalem is spread out like a map below the eye on one hand, and on the other is a wide and dreary horizon of desert country – the Moab Mountains, the Valley of the Jordan and the Dead Sea; and still nearer, the wild hills, volcanic-looking, tinted with bright arid hues, through which runs the road to Jericho, as unsafe now as in the time when it furnished the appropriate scene of the parable of the 'Good Samaritan.'[81]

Bartlett wrote two other books about the Holy Land: *Footsteps of our Lord and His Apostles* (1851) and *Jerusalem Revisited*, which was published posthumously in 1855. Like *Walks*, these include steel engravings and woodcuts to illustrate the author's travels. Both books contain material which Bartlett had published previously, sometimes verbatim and sometimes rewritten. *Footsteps*, for example, includes details of his journeys to the East in 1834, 1837, and 1842. Because of the way in which the author moves backwards and forwards in time and place in this book, the narrative is sometimes confused, especially when Bartlett mixes his own travels in with those of the Apostle Paul.

As with *Walks*, the best writing in *Footsteps* comes when Bartlett, free from history and contemporary debate, is giving descriptions of the landscape he sees. The ascent of the Mount of Olives now contains additions in a style recalling Lamartine:

Looking back, Bethany is seen nestling below in its dark covert of trees, overhung by the hills of the desert, hot, brown, and indescribably desolate, – a wilderness of jagged, red, and yellow peaks, shapeless and horrid. Overtopping them all is the distant range of the Moab Mountains. Who, that has been at Jerusalem, but remembers their peculiar pink and violet colouring, intense beyond conception in our neutral-tinted country! Now come the olives, thinly scattered over the sacred hill, some evidently very ancient; their trunks are generally twisted about fantastically, – their straggling roots dive in between the clefts of rocks, or, void of earthy covering, project, skeleton like, out of the stony ground. Their foliage is thin and sombre, the oval leaf a dark dull green above, and silvery beneath, and there is a peculiar sadness in their low soft rustle when agitated by the gusty breeze. A shepherd or two in a brown striped dress, and legs and face still browner, is seated at the foot of one of these grey trunks, and a flock of goats, with long and silken hair, of dark brown, glossy bluish black, dull yellow, or white, is scattered about the arid, rocky soil.[82]

This prose should be set alongside other excerpts less strained and more natural. One of the best, because it reveals something of the artist's humour under rather trying conditions, is the description of the ship that is to take him from Alexandria to Jaffa: 'Our vessel was just like the old models in nautical cabinets of ships in the middle ages, high tilted at the poop and stern, and with masts, spars, and rigging of curious and antique fashion. So far so good – to a lover of the picturesque; but this was not all; the craft was perilously crazy, the seams yawned as if the shrunken planks were about to come asunder, the ropes and sails looked as if the first stiff breeze would snap the one and split the others to shreds and tatters. There was neither chart nor compass on board. It was, in fact, just a sample of the Arab coasting vessels, the wrecks of which so picturesquely bestrew the shores of Syria.'[83]

Bartlett on many other occasions showed himself capable of assessing and distinguishing what was real and what was picturesque. He seldom failed to realize that many of his picturesque views were linked with suffering and appalling human misery whether it was in Acre, Damascus, Jerusalem, Athens, or Syracuse.[84] In Jerusalem he noted the hovels which the poor inhabited on the edge of the Jewish quarter and the appearance of 'their straggling tenants, who carried privation and sickliness in their pallid countenances'; he quotes from

Dr Macgowan's report of 1843 to the London Society for Promoting Christianity among the Jews that the poor class lives in ' ... dark vaulted caves, the roof dripping with damp from above, and the bare earth beneath, and often without door or window to keep out the wind and rain ... a miserable existence ... The want of attendance, of cleanliness, of suitable nourishment, and of ordinary precautions, is quite appalling.'[85] Bartlett himself recognized that the tourist in search of the picturesque could and often did ignore what was really significant:

The fashionable traveller, on the other hand, satiate with the charms of Italy, weary of the Alps and the Black Forest, seeks Oriental excitement and western civilization on the banks of the Nile, or the desolate hills of Judea, and lisps out his disappointment that there are no trees or water in Jerusalem, while the hotels are *very* inferior. He rails at the fanaticism which excludes him from the only pretty spot (the mosque enclosure), and boasts, that two days 'have done the Mount of Olives, the Wailing Place, Bethlehem, the Greek Fire, and all that.' Such persons leave the Holy City without a suspicion of the earnest men and women who have here found a home and heart-stirring employment, where vacancy and ennui enter not.[86]

The best of the engravings and woodcuts in *Walks*, *Footsteps*, and *Jerusalem Revisited* appear in the second edition of *Walks*, which contains twenty-two full-page prints. In the other two books the illustrations are usually of vignette size. Eighteen Bartlett engravings of the East also appear in Conybeare and Howson's *Life and Epistles of St. Paul*, the first volume of which was published in 1850 and the second in 1853. Of the eastern sketches, those in *Walks*, second edition, of the 'Lower Pool of Gihon, Jerusalem' (p. 56), 'Enclosure of the Temple, Jerusalem' (p. 143), 'Church of the Holy Sepulchre' (p. 168); and those in *Life and Epistles of St. Paul* of 'Tarsus' (I, 52), 'Piraeus' (I, 374), 'Mitylene' (II, 216), 'Rhodes' (II, 231), and 'Acre' (II, 237), are very good examples of Bartlett's work. Two at the western end of St Paul's journey also deserve mention: 'Syracuse' (II, 358) and 'Rome' (II, 427).

Two other books by Bartlett belong to the East: *Forty Days in the Desert* (1848) and *The Nile Boat* (1849). These two volumes were the outcome of his travels in August–September 1845, when he journeyed seven hundred miles up the Nile to the temple of Philæ above Assuan, and October–December 1845, when he travelled along the east side of the Gulf of Suez to Mount Serbal, then east to the Gulf of Akaba, and north to Petra. Both books rely heavily on the work of historians like Sir Gardner Wilkinson and Samuel Sharpe, who wrote the introduction to *The Nile Boat*; on Léon Laborde's *Un artiste dans le desert*, *souvenirs d'Orient* (1839); and on the research of Dr Richard Lepsius in Egypt and the Sinai. Lepsius supported the theory that Mount Serbal was the Mount Sinai of Mosaic times.

In his Preface to *The Nile Boat*, Bartlett disclaims for the text 'any pretensions to originality' other than that possessed by his illustrations, which 'were drawn upon the spot, many of them with the Camera Lucida.' Much the same could be said of *Forty Days in the Desert*, although 'the special objects' which justified it were different: ' ... to give somewhat more of distinctness to the route of the Israelites than is to be found in the work of Laborde; to depict, though but imperfectly, the valley of Feiran, and the neighbouring mountain of the Serbal, not only the most romantic spot in the Arabian peninsula, but confidently pronounced by no less a *savant* than Dr. Lepsius to be the real Sinai; as also to give a picture of Petra, that extraordinary rock-hewn capital of Edom, which, by its singular wildness, even yet seems, beyond any other place, to thrill the imagination, and waken the love of adventure.'[87]

In spite of Bartlett's modesty about the originality and even the value of his writing, there is ample evidence to indicate that his books were popular with the public. By 1862 both *Forty Days in the Desert* and *The Nile Boat* had run to five editions. In 1872 Bell and Daldy of Covent Garden brought out the seventh edition of *Footsteps of Our Lord and His Apostles*.

Forty Days and *The Nile Boat* were successful, not because of any lack of material about their subject matter or any waning of mid-Victorian interest in Biblical exegesis, but because they were books which read easily and were interesting both for the sixty small steel engravings and numerous woodcuts which accompanied the text and for the prose style which had become more flexible and personal. Furthermore, the author's itinerary up the Nile and across the Sinai imposed limits upon his writing, ensuring a greater unity and coherence than in earlier works. Throughout these two books Bartlett's commonsense, his appreciation of the differences underlying the picturesque and the realistic, his humour and humanity, offset his religiosity and the cloying vestiges of Romanticism.

As he prepared to leave Cairo he commented humorously upon the clothing he should take with him and remarked that 'a clean shirt is not without its moral effect even in the wilderness, and among people whose linen looks as if it had come down unwashed from the days of Ishmael.'[88] Of the members of his little caravan he was touched by the plight of ' ... one little fellow whom I came to regard, at last, with attachment; a limber slip of a boy about twelve years of age, delicate and spare, and apparently quite unequal to the fatigue and exposure of a long journey over the burning Desert. But one might see that from the lap of his Bedouin mother his life had been one of hardship and privation; his bones almost protruded through his soft and dusky skin, worn and rubbed white at the salient angles, with hard labour, like those of a negro.'[89]

Again and again the printed words in *Forty Days* assume as much power as the engravings: 'Plain, mountain, and wady in a blaze of white heat, "lie like a load on the weary eye," and seem as if they had just passed, all palpitating, through a fiery crucible.'[90] We see cannon that had 'dozed into the rust of untold years'; a stores laden camel obstinately running away in a blinding desert storm; the corpse of a poor Fellah, who had fled through the sands of Sinai, after the defeat of Ibrahim Pasha's army by the English at Acre; 'the Mahmal, or camel selected to carry, under a costly canopy, the copy of the Koran sent to Mecca'; and 'the foul dens where the unhappy insane' of Cairo were put on display before the reforms of Mehemet Ali.

The same vivid word pictures abound in *The Nile Boat*. Outside Cairo's Gate of Victory 'high mounds of rubbish conceal the tops of minarets' belonging to the tombs of the Memlook Sultans, which 'backed by hills of an aspect wildly desolate ... "rise like an exhalation" from the blanching waste.'[91] We have the 'distressing spectacle' of 'meagre listless infants, covered with dirt and flies, which form a black ring around their apparently weak diseased eyes';[92] and the 'melancholy sameness' of the 'wretched mud villages and small towns, built amid raised mounds of rubbish and filth which the wind scatters in clouds into every cranny of the place.'[93] We have, too, Bartlett's adventure in the 'spacious and splendid marble paved' Damascus house where he sees the 'laughing black eyes' of the ladies of the harem whom the elderly Moolah 'gravely drove back ... as some old pedagogue would a bevy of noisy romps' so that the artist could sketch his favourite wife. There is the embarrassing moment when Bartlett with his 'Frank hat and umbrella' is hoisted up on a platform to a seat of honour to observe 'the unveiled grossness' of the Ghawazee or dancing girls, 'who, banished from the capital, were forced to carry their voluptuous entertainment' farther up the Nile. There is also the occasion when Bartlett, witnessing a 'fat, flabby old Turk' negotiating for the purchase of an Abyssinian girl, contrasts slavery in Egypt and America: 'Egypt, fallen and decrepit, bowed under oppression and the paralysing influence of a false religion. America, daily rising in power, a land of light, freedom, enterprise, and Christianity! By what extraordinary chance is it then, that unlike in everything else, they should resemble each other only in one damning particular ... '⁹⁴

It is word pictures such as these that claim the attention of the reader today rather than the author's sublime description of the 'the stupendous magnitude and almost overwhelming grandeur' of both the Pyramids and Niagara Falls 'when you stand close beneath them.'

But no matter 'how beautifully illustrated and elegantly finished' they were, the public demand for travel books of the East continued to decline. In its 1852 review of *Footsteps of our Lord and His Apostles*, *Tait's Edinburgh Magazine* was decidedly querulous: 'Once more the East! the everlasting East! that standing dish of literary cookery, which is for ever being served up, till it ceases to gratify the mental palate or nourish the intellectual stomach ... Let us suppose we read, say for instance, only a few of these all but daily Oriental productions. Alas! We have read them all! Yes; there they are: the same Arabs, camels, deserts, tombs and jackals that we journeyed with, rode on, traversed, dived into and cursed respectively, only a week ago, with some other traveller.' The reviewer maintained 'seriously' that there was 'a little too much book-making in this once sacred, now fashionable quarter.' Having praised the book's physical appearance, the best the reviewer could do was to say that *Footsteps* was 'amusing,' and that the author's reputation 'as an artist should secure it a place, if not in the library, at least in the drawing-room or boudoir.' Such reviews – even if few in number – help explain why Bartlett turned to the less exciting but more reliable life of a journalist from March 1849 to January 1852.

Literature had always appealed to him and his knowledge of English literature was very considerable. It is on occasion hard to say whether, given a choice, Bartlett would have elected art or letters as his vocation. One suspects, however, that his acceptance of the editorship of *Sharpe's London Journal* in 1849 was more a matter of economic necessity than it was of deliberate choice. But there may have been a considerable satisfaction, too, for the post meant that Bartlett could enjoy 'his own cheerful hearth' and be with his children, a happiness which Beattie says he 'too seldom enjoyed.' The eldest, John Spencer, was now fourteen while the youngest, Helen, was just a year old. That he took his position with Victorian seriousness is obvious from even a cursory examination of the volumes that appeared under his management. His *Journal* was to set a 'good example' by 'diffusing valuable information blended with harmless amusement' and such as would 'act as an antidote to the deluge of demoralizing literature, the statistics of which are frightful, and which has for its object the subversion of all religion, morality and government.'[95]

Under the heading 'Editor's Writing-Desk,' or 'Reviews,' Bartlett reviewed a wide variety of books from the press. Not all the reviews are signed, but it seems reasonable to assume that Bartlett wrote most if not all of them; they included such books as Beattie's *The Life and Letters of Thomas Campbell*, Dixon's *John Howard: and the Prison World of Europe in the Eighteenth Century*, Ruskin's *The Seven Lamps of Architecture*, Britton's *Autobiography*, Kingley's *Alton Locke*, Conybeare and Howson's *Life and Epistles of St. Paul*, Miller's *Footprints of the Creator*, Charlotte Brontë's *Shirley*, Tennyson's *In Memoriam*, Leigh Hunt's *Autobiography*, Wordsworth's *Prelude*. The reviews themselves are not penetrating but do reveal that Bartlett read the books conscientiously and tried to make his readers aware of their content. Many concern popular novels and books of poetry now forgotten. Others indicate the reviewer's own limitations or bias: Herman Melville's *Mardi and the Voyage Thither* 'is a difficult book to describe, because it aims at many things and achieves none satisfactorily ... a preaching of certain transcendental nonsense ... '; Ruskin is reprimanded for 'depreciating the glorious achievement of the present'; Hugh Miller is praised for 'the services' he renders to 'Theology and Geology' and William Wordsworth for 'the lessons of virtue which it was his grand aim to inculcate'; Charlotte Brontë's *Jane Eyre* suffers from the author's error 'in making a woman and a heroine ... such that her sex disowns her – nay, will even blush for her'; Tennyson's *In Memoriam* 'abounds with noble aspirations and generous sentiments which reflect equal glory on the philanthropist and the poet ... '

Both Agnes Strickland and Catherine Parr Traill wrote articles and stories for *Sharpe's London Journal*. Mary Cowden Clarke's series on characters of Shakespeare's plays ran for several numbers. Travel items were favourites with the readers, and steel engravings often accompanied the text. Novels in serial form were a regular feature, one of the most popular being Francis Edward Smedley's *Lewis Arundel; or, The Railroad of Life*.

Nearly every issue included an item on art, often a critique of an engraving. 'The Banditti' from a picture by Cattermole drew an interesting comment from the editor, who maintained that the artist 'may almost be called the English Salvator Rosa' in that 'his *penchant* is for the delineation of the sombre, although he affects rather the picturesquely gloomy in architecture than the savagely grand in Nature.'[96] The critiques are nearly always favourable and intended to introduce the artist and his work to the public. Sometimes the old and contemporary are juxtaposed. In an article on Venice the editor praises Canaletto and admits his uneasiness about the work of Prout and Turner: 'For who has not seen innumerable paintings and engravings of every object of interest within her confines? – the pictures by Canaletto, of St. Mark's Place, and the Rialto, and canal scenes by the thousand, all true and exact to a touch, even to the very greenish colour and ripple of the water; besides the more brilliant, but less faithful works of Prout, and the fantastic and gorgeous idealities of Turner; (which, in spite of the authority of the "Oxford Graduate" [John Ruskin], we must maintain, beautiful as they are, to be about as unlike the actual Venice as possible).'[97]

During his time as editor of *Sharpe's London Journal*, Bartlett prepared the text for the handsome folio volume, *The Wilkie Gallery*. According to the *Art-Journal* of February 1850, George Virtue had just published Part 17 of this biography of Sir David Wilkie, RA, which contained forty-four steel engravings (9 × 6 inch) of Wilkie's paintings. For each of the engravings Bartlett wrote a 'critical notice' explaining the circumstances described in the picture and the merits of the composition.

The criticism is nearly always laudatory, and Bartlett makes no serious effort to evaluate Wilkie's domestic portraiture in terms, for example, of the qualities of Dutch genre painting but instead limits himself to the comment that Wilkie 'had a natural and corresponding sympathy' for 'etchings from the works of Rembrandt and Ostade.'[98] Sometimes his remarks seem to lack critical sense as when he quotes Wilkie on Vandyke's painting of children and then offers extravagant praise of Wilkie's indifferently executed 'The Senorita and her Nurse': 'There is an old proverb that "the French are wiser than they seem, and the Spanish look wiser than they are." The sketch before us may well be called *delicious*, for its perfect comprehension of this peculiarity of the national character, as well as for its vivid look of life; and its airy, graceful, and masterly style of handling.' Of the 'Daughter of Admiral Walker,' Bartlett remarks that 'none but a great artist could throw off, apparently without an effort, a work so consummate in feeling, and so ethereal and graceful in touch and handling. There is, if we may use such a word, a sort of inspiration about it.' It is difficult to realize that Bartlett could make such judgments when he must have seen the portraits of children by artists like Vandyke, Gainsborough, Reynolds, and Hogarth.

It may well be argued that Bartlett is too deeply committed to the 'fine moral tone' of middle class Victorian sensibility; he thinks, for instance, of the 'works of Wilkie' circulating 'among all classes of the community' to produce 'a taste for art' and to exercise 'refining and humanizing influences.'⁹⁹ But even granting his commitment to the Christian morality of his time and his admiration for Wilkie's 'kindliness, simplicity, purity, and benevolence of heart,' it is somewhat dismaying to find in his writing such a lack of critical taste.

Although William Beattie lists *The Wilkie Gallery* as a work written by W.H. Bartlett, it should be noted that the author's name does not appear in this book. Only an indirect reference makes the writer's identity apparent. This reference is in an essay near the end of the book in connection with the engraving of 'A Group of Camels at Smyrna'; for his essay 'the writer' extracts two paragraphs from his *Forty Days in the Desert* and places them under the heading 'Camel Riding' and 'The Caravan.' It would be helpful to know what kind of agreement Bartlett had with his publisher when he undertook this anonymous work.

Another small volume, *Scripture Sites and Scenes ... in Egypt, Arabia, and Palestine* (1849), belongs to this period. The Introduction explains that the object of the book was 'to give to the Bible student, and especially the youthful reader, distinct and truthful ideas' of some of the 'hallowed scenes' of biblical history. It contained a map of Palestine and nineteen engravings selected from *Walks*, *Forty Days*, and *The Nile Boat*. Each engraving has a few paragraphs of descriptive comment to help the student understand its significance. By November 1854 a new edition of this volume was in the press.

The popularity of Bartlett's illustrations of the Holy Land was brought to the attention of Londoners during the summer of 1851 when the 'Great Diorama of Jerusalem and the Holy Land' was exhibited in St George's Gallery, Hyde Park Corner, within easy distance of the Great Exhibition and the Crystal Palace. The 'Diorama' was described as having life-size figures 'forming a Series of Moving Pictures on an unequalled Scale of Magnitude and Grandeur.' It was painted by a Mr W. Beverly 'from sketches, made on the spot, during repeated journeys in the East, by Mr W.H. Bartlett.' The *Evangelical Magazine* of July 1851 concluded its praise of 'The Great Diorama' in these words: 'We earnestly advise all lovers of the Bible who live in London or who may visit our great City in this eventful year, to repair to this Diorama of Jerusalem and the Holy Land. A more rational and instructive hour they cannot spend; and if they can retire from the affecting spectacle without shedding tears, as they gaze upon "the Jews' Place of Wailing," they will be made of sterner stuff than we can boast.' This 'unique and tasteful exhibition' was made even more attractive for the public by 'accompanying music' and an 'efficient choir' that sang selections from sacred music under the direction of Mr J.H. Tully at the organ.

VII

In the spring of 1850 Bartlett travelled with his son by way of Paris and Marseilles to Malta and then to Gibraltar, whence they paid a visit to Malaga and Granada. These travels are described in *Gleanings, Pictorial and Antiquarian, on the Overland Route*, which was published in 1851. It is not as satisfactory a work as *The Nile Boat* or *Forty Days* because it could, as Bartlett admits in the Preface, pretend to no originality, hundreds of books and engravings having already appeared on the subject of which it treats.' It lacks the Bartlett anecdotes, which add so much to the interest of the two earlier books. Much of the book is a historical account of the rise and fall of the Order of the Knights Hospitallers of St John together with that of the Templars. Chapter II has a brief account of the Hospitallers' occupation of the Island of Rhodes where Bartlett had remained for a month in 1834 recovering from a serious fever that nearly claimed his life while he was sailing between Tarsus and Rhodes (B115). The next chapter gives a detailed description of spots in Malta 'rendered famous by the heroism of La Valetta and his Knights.' Chapter IV is a 'dissertation' on the Apostle Paul's voyage and shipwreck on Malta,[100] and chapters V and VI an account of the ruins of Hagiar Chem and the voyage from Malta to Gibraltar. Chapter VII contains a 'topographical and historical sketch of Gibraltar,' where Bartlett landed at the end of March 1850, having on the way put in for a day at Tunis, where he walked over the ancient fields of Carthage. The numerous sieges which threatened the 'Rock' are recounted and the various bastions and batteries described and even sketched once permission was given. Although the references are from secondary sources, Bartlett's historical narrative is interesting enough to hold the reader's attention in a way that escapes the ability of many better qualified historians.

The 'excursion' to Granada forms an interesting chapter of the book because so much of it is based upon Bartlett's own observations. In Malaga, 'one of the least interesting places in Spain' in spite of its 'Elysian' spring climate, the party which included the author, his son, 'a clergyman and his lady, and a young friend,' hired six horses, beasts that 'looked much like lineal descendants of Rosinante' and set out 'on horseback for Granada and its Alhambra.' The guide was ' ... a singular-looking ecclesiastic, who, dressed in the usual costume of his order, might have passed for Sancho himself in canonicals. His intellectual regions were rather pinched, the top of his head being narrow, and gradually widening into a broad round face, terminating in an immense amplitude of jaw and chin.'[101]

Granada's Moorish architecture impressed Bartlett so much that he quoted at length from Washington Irving's 'inimitable descriptions' contained in *The Alhambra* in order that his readers would be informed about 'the prominent points in the history' of the Moors. Like Irving, Bartlett much admired the Alhambra, which he found especially romantic at night: ' ... by haunting it on the moonlight nights ... we fully realized all that is magical in this fairy palace ... when the play of the light and shade among these avenues of Arabesque pillars was most fantastic and startling, the shadows of the halls more vast and sombre – when the sleeping Albaycin, with its Moorish houses and courts below, was bathed in pale white light, and the outstretched Vega and its mountain barrier dimly descried through the silvery haze of night.'[102]

The twenty-eight steel engravings for the *Overland Route* appear one to a page and are in vignette form. The most attractive are the street scenes in Valetta and Rhodes and the view of Granada on the frontispiece. Although the Preface suggests that the 'Overland Route' referred to in the title is the one to India and that the book will give 'correct and graphic pictures of a few prominent objects either on or bordering upon it,' the reader is confined to the Mediterranean and, in particular, to Malta, Gibraltar, and Granada. The Appendix gives some details about steamship connections to Suez, Bombay, Calcutta, and China and warns the reader that the author's information 'to the traveller, after leaving Suez, is but second-hand' and that 'there is little on his way worthy of attention until his arrival on the coast of India'!

The last of Bartlett's European travel books, *Pictures from Sicily*, which was in press late in 1852, was based largely upon his visit to the island in the spring and summer of that year. A short historical Introduction of thirty-four pages provides the reader with a thumbnail sketch of 'only the most remarkable events of ancient times.' The reader then accompanies Bartlett to the island by express train from Paris to Châlons-sur-Saône, by steamer to Lyons, by diligence from Valence to Avignon, where he took the train for Marseilles. A mail boat then conveyed him to Ajaccio in Corsica and to Leghorn, where he made excursions to Pisa and Florence and observed that Mr Ruskin has written 'in a strain of rather overwrought enthusiasm' about the Campanile of Giotto. A French steamer carried him on to Naples, where he climbed Vesuvius, and gazed upon 'the awful abyss of the crater ... its sides scorched and blasted by the action of the fire, and coloured alternatively in black, red, and yellow veins.' At Pompeii, which he had visited previously, Bartlett felt 'the lifeless melancholy of the excavated city,' and expressed his amazement at the 'minute dimensions' of the shops and houses 'literally too small to swing a cat in' and wonders 'how the inhabitants could have stowed themselves away.'

About half way through the book, Bartlett has entered the Straits of Messina and is informing his reader of the earthquake which shook Messina on 26 February of that same year. From Messina the route is to Catania, with a side trip to Etna, then on to Syracuse, Agrigento, Sciacca, and Castelvetrano, at which point the direction is across the country to Salemi and Calatafimi so that Bartlett can see the 'most majestic vision' of the temple of Segeste ' ... standing in lonely sublimity on a lofty precipice, surrounded by an amphitheatre of craggy mountains, closed in by the graceful peaks of Eryx.' Palermo and its environs are carefully described and its history referred to in some detail. By mid-August Bartlett was back in England where he read an account in *The Times* of the eruption of Etna on 20 August.[103]

Although the style is uneven, *Pictures from Sicily* is a more attractive book visually than the *Overland Route* because of the variety of its thirty-three engraved illustrations. Sicily offered Bartlett the kind of panoramas which he liked: Messina and the Faro, Nicolosi, the approach to Agrigento, Segeste, and the view from the Victoria Hotel at Palermo. In addition, there were splendid views of ancient ruins: the theatre at Taormina, the Temple of Concord at Agrigento, and the amphitheatre of Syracuse. To vary the offering of prospects and classical ruins, Bartlett included pictures of the well at Catania, the Ear of Dionysius at Syracuse, the Cathedral and the Convent Gate at Palermo. These illustrations in vignette form, together with sixteen woodcuts, helped ensure that *Pictures from Sicily* continued to be printed long after the appearance of the first edition.

Bartlett realized, however, that developments in travel and communications were effecting profound social changes and that these in turn had already created special problems for authors interested in picturesque description:

... in these days of railroads and submarine telegraphs, there is no excuse for lingering a moment to describe what is familiar to everybody. And with a full appreciation of the value of railroads, not only in social and economical aspects, but also to the traveller, in abridging vast spaces of comparatively uninteresting country, and planting him, with a vast saving of time and trouble, at the very spot he desires to visit, it is certain that they are sad levellers of impressions, and make all countries look very much alike.[104]

The picturesque travel book had depended in large measure for its popularity upon difficulty rather than ease of travel. By 1853 travel was reasonably easy and pleasant for all those members of society who had so regularly purchased George Virtue's illustrated travel books, with the partial consequence that the demand for such books was now less. For the author the problem was to find scenery which was not already 'familiar to everybody.' Sicily's lack of rail transportation and her bad inland roads did mean that in this island the author in search of the picturesque could still find much to interest readers at home. But Bartlett knew that such opportunities were now very limited. Some other use had to be found for his talents.

As he grew older his interests had centred increasingly on history for which his sketches of old buildings and ancient ruins made admirable illustrations. Even a sketch of a contemporary landscape could do much to help a reader envisage a historical event. For this reason Dr James Taylor used twenty Bartlett scenes in his *Pictorial History of Scotland*, 1852–9, to show his readers such battlefields as Bannockburn, Killiecrankie, Preston Pans, Falkirk, and Bothwell Bridge. One of the most interesting of the engravings is that of 'The Grassmarket, Edinburgh' (II, 708), which reveals a busy street against the sunlit facade of old shops with the hill and Castle in the background.

In 1853 Bartlett offered his reading public his own illustrated history book, *The Pilgrim Fathers; or the Founders of New England*, on the grounds that the details of the Puritan emigration were 'almost unknown to the mass of English readers.' The book was dedicated to Dr William Beattie 'in grateful acknowledgement of his unvarying kindness during a period of more than twenty years.' The illustrations comprised twenty-eight engravings on steel and thirty-one woodcuts after Bartlett sketches; it is 'from these pen-and-pencil memorials,' Bartlett comments, 'and these alone, that [my] work can lay claim to any distinctive originality.'[105] He lists his sources in the Preface, telling his readers that his objective is 'to compress the scattered particulars of the tale into a continuous narrative.'

The first half of the book explains the origin of the Puritans and traces their vicissitudes from the time of their separation from the established Church of England and the setting up of their own places of worship to their flight to Holland and their eventual departure from Delfthaven and Southampton. This part of the history has interesting woodcuts of the Town Hall at Leyden; Emmanuel College, Cambridge; and Standish Church. The steel engravings are on the whole not as effective as those in *Pictures from Sicily*. The carefully toned 'Doorway' of Austerfield Church, the moonlit landscape of Scrooby, the architecturally correct drawings of the church and town hall at Boston, and of the 'Jerusalem Hof' and the 'Old Gates' at Leyden are, however, good illustrations.

Although historical events make up the matter of this book, Bartlett's prose is often vivid because of his acquaintance with places linked closely to his history. Boston in England becomes something more interesting than the 'centre of a rich agricultural and grazing district':

It was a brilliant morning when we arrived, and the crowded market-place, with its quaint antique houses, overlooked by the tall tower of the church, strongly reminded one of the picturesque cities of Flanders. The streets were all in a swarm with broad-shouldered bull-headed farmers, of the true old breed, and their rosy-cheeked comely wives and daughters bustling about at the grocers' and haberdashers'. Itinerant auctioneers, perched on stalls, were putting up the most splendid bargains of gay-coloured waistcoats and brass buttons, and dresses of flaming patterns for the girls. The doorways of the inns swarmed with the burly race, mighty in their potations, and the court-yards were crammed with rusty old gigs and carts, in which they had repaired from their farms. Once a-week the town is thus aroused from the drowsy quietude of an old decayed place.[106]

Bartlett's interest in local behavior in one of the 'primitive country taverns'[107] of the 'go-a-head' United States provides the reader with passages that lighten the tale of Indian treachery and Puritan seriousness: 'At half-past five, the bell is rung, to arouse the inmates from sleep, and another at six summons them to breakfast. This is spread in a long bare looking room, where the boarders – most of them working men or journeymen, a few travellers, with possibly one or two of a higher grade in society – assemble at the table, which is decently though not

71

luxuriously spread. No words are wasted and no time is lost, and in ten minutes the meal is over, and the apartment empty. Dinner at noon, and tea at six, are performed with the same despatch and silence ... '[108] On another occasion in Plymouth, after supper, Bartlett observed ' ... a beautiful little girl about twelve, deeply engaged in the perusal of a book, which I asked her to allow me to look at, supposing it might be perhaps *Robinson Crusoe*, or *Sandford and Merton*, if not a work of a still more edifying tendency. But oh – Shades of the Pilgrims – what was my consternation! when, with a beaming countenance, she presented me with the *Mysteries of Paris*, exclaiming withal, "that it was a very pretty book, and *had only one murder in it!*" '[109] He concluded that the incident 'showed how wide a revolution in the state of the community must have happened since Pilgrim days.' *Sharpe's London Journal* may have had a limited circulation on the Cape!

The engravings in the second half of the book with one or two exceptions are usually empty landscapes. Even Provincetown seems pale and uninteresting. Many of the woodcuts in this part of the book represent typical household effects or memorials of early settlement; two or three of these woodcuts are more satisfying than some of the steel engravings.

As the Preface states, the book 'has no theological purpose or predilection.' It is an attractive history of an heroic emigration which today has added significance because of our interest in what Bartlett had to report when, in 1852, after an eleven-day voyage from Liverpool and a two- or three-hour trip on the Old Colony Railroad from Boston, he found himself in Plymouth, New England.

Twenty-three of the original sketches for *The Pilgrim Fathers* and for *Pictures from Sicily* were bound in a folio which also contains seven original sketches for *Jerusalem Revisited* and one for *Walks about the City and Environs of Jerusalem*. Altogether there may be thirty-eight original Bartletts in this volume.[110] Of the sketches, one is a panorama (pencil and sepia of Leyden), twenty-six are sepia washes, three are in pencil, and eight are sepia on a blue sketching paper. Seven of these may never have been engraved as they do not seem to have appeared in any publication. The most interesting of these is the 'View from Boston Tower' in England. The folio bears a bookplate indicating that it came from the library of George Henry Virtue, FSA, elder son of George Virtue (1793?–1868) whose publishing business in London owed a good deal of its success to the illustrations which Bartlett provided for the many elegant volumes which came from its presses. The folio was handsomely bound – presumably by the Virtue firm – and entitled on the spine, *Original Drawings by W.H. Bartlett*. Many questions come to mind about this volume. Was it sold after the owner's death in 1866? Were there other volumes like it which were purchased by art dealers, who then sold the sketches separately? Are any other such folios in existence? Why were these drawings not sold after Bartlett's death?

In December 1855 *The Art-Journal* called its readers' attention to the 'very large collection' of Bartlett drawings that were to be sold by Messrs Southgate and Barrett, Fleet Street, London. The *Journal*'s account was detailed and informative:

... in the sale will be drawings made in Switzerland, Ireland, Scotland, Canada, the United States, various parts of England, on the Bosphorus and the Danube, in the Holy Land, and in several other countries in the Old and New Worlds. It is worthy of remark that the authenticity of the whole will be guaranteed: for they are all the original drawings made for the several works published during the last twenty years by Mr. Virtue ... It will be readily understood, that the series, which number several hundreds, are greatly varied in subject and character: they are for the most part highly interesting, as true copies of the most attractive scenery of Europe, Asia, and America, as illustrations of national manners and costumes, or as portraits of structures inseparably linked with memorable associations: we cannot doubt, therefore, the peculiar attractions of the sale.

Virtue and Company printed a *Catalogue* for the sale[111] which omitted any mention of the drawings made in Canada or the United States. Presumably these were omitted because they had been sold privately. The *Catalogue* listed 205 lots which contained altogether 1012 items. Of these 517 were described as 'original sepia drawings'; 125 were listed as 'original water-colour and sepia drawings'; and 370 were described as 'original water-colour drawings,' about one-half of all the drawings that were sold. The sale realized £277.4.0., a rather pathetic figure when one thinks of the prices asked for original Bartletts today.

Because the *Catalogue* omits Bartlett drawings in such works as *Picturesque Antiquities of the English Cities, Ireland Illustrated, Devonshire and Cornwall Illustrated, The Watering Places of Great Britain and Fashionable Directory, American Scenery, Canadian Scenery, The Pilgrim Fathers*, and *Pictures from Sicily*, it is reasonable to assume that Bartlett must have made more than 1500 sketches between 1824 and 1854. Other artists have sketched or painted much more within such a time period, but very few travelled so far and under such trying conditions, and few combined the work of artist and author as effectively

73

as did Bartlett. An interesting parallel might be Edward Lear (1812–1888). The parallel extends even to the sort of scenery which inspired the two men. Speaking of Calabria on 25 July 1847, Lear is moved to exclaim: 'But – Calabria! – No sooner is the word uttered than a new world arises before the mind's eye, – torrents, fastnesses, all the prodigality of mountain scenery, – caves, brigands, and pointed hats, – Mrs Radcliffe and Salvator Rosa, – costumes and character, – horrors and magnificence without end.'[112] Both Lear and Bartlett travelled extensively, both were topographical artists, both could write imaginatively about their travels, and both were shy, lonely men. And though he wrote no poetry, Bartlett would surely have enjoyed reading *The Book of Nonsense* to his youngest children at Highgate in 1846.

Although Beattie refers to *The Pilgrim Fathers*, he makes no reference, except in his bibliography, to *The History of the United States of America*, to which Bartlett contributed the first three books – over one-quarter of the 2144 pages which made up the three large volumes. The *History*, completed by B.B. Woodward and published in June 1856, two years after Bartlett's death, contained thirty-one Bartlett engravings from *American Scenery* and one from *Canadian Scenery*.

The first three books trace events from the earliest discoveries in North America to Cornwallis's surrender at Yorktown in 1781. Much of the narrative is schoolboy history in which the emphasis is upon the exciting and often bloody events of colonial wars. Unlike B.B. Woodward, Bartlett is content just to tell the story, although he does sometimes make interesting observations that quite transcend the historical detail that too often clouds his purpose. After the British declaration of war on the Dutch in 1781 that followed the capture of Henry Laurens, Bartlett turns, for example, to consider the wider conflict in these words: 'In the West Indies, at the rock of Gibraltar, even in the distant Hindostan [*sic*], the English, though at a ruinous expense, met and eventually triumphed over their European enemies, and the origin of the war was almost forgotten amidst the vast and increasing hostilities which it had called into existence.'[113] If there is a bias, it is in favour of the Americans; if the history falls short of being significant, it is because Bartlett relies too much on secondary sources, which fill his own narrative with pages of factual material: the events of military campaigns, the horrors of Indian massacres, and biographical details of minor figures. Cause and result are blurred over by the happenings, and the reader is too often compelled to provide his own transitions and conclusions and to guess at motives. It is a history that all too clearly reveals the author's shortcomings as a historian.

Bartlett's own travels in America, however, helped him sustain a realistic narrative as he moved about on rivers like the Hudson, the Delaware, the Potomac, and the St Lawrence. He had an accurate knowledge of the topography of cities like Montreal and Quebec and of the waterways which linked them to Boston and New York. He had, furthermore, the sort of detailed acquaintance with sections of the eastern seaboard which made it a fairly simple matter for him to describe, for example, the campaign manœuvres of Washington, Howe, and Cornwallis.

Occasionally his love of the picturesque triumphed and history waited upon him:

But one should see Quebec in winter, fully to appreciate its picturesque peculiarities. From the heights of the citadel, the eye then rests upon what seems one boundless lake of milk; all irregularities of ground, fences, boundaries, and copsewoods are obliterated; the tops of villages, with their Catholic steeples, from which the bell booms plaintive and solitary through the wintry air, and scattered farms, peep up like islets in an ocean, with here and there dark lines of pine-forest, the mast of some ice-locked schooner, or the curling smoke of a solitary Indian wigwam. The town has its strange dark gables and pointed roofs all relieved with the lustrous white snow; its rugged streets are one day choked with heaped-up ice and drift, and, upon a slight thaw, flooded with dirty kennels and miniature cascades, which the next frost converts into a dangerous and slippery surface. Cloth or carpet boots, goloshes with spikes to their heels, iron-pointed walking sticks, are the only weapons defensive against broken limbs and necks ... That branch of the river to the north of the Isle of Orleans is always frozen over ... In general, however, the main channel remains open, and encumbered with vast masses of ice; and a strange sight it is, to see the dexterous and fearless boatmen striving with iron-pointed poles to raise their vessels upon the surface of these floating ice-bergs, and thus descend the stream with them, till they find open water on which to launch their barks anew upon the troubled and perilous flood.[114]

Although *The History of the United States of America* is never likely to be consulted by scholars or even general readers, it remains evidence of Bartlett's impressive energy, an energy which kept him writing, sketching, and travelling to the day of his death in 1854. The *History* does, however, raise at least one difficult question about Bartlett's travels in America. When did he see Quebec in the depths of winter? As there seems to be no record of where he spent the winter of 1836–7, it is interesting to speculate on his whereabouts at that time. The account of Quebec in winter may, of course, be based upon his memory of the city in other seasons and upon descriptions given by other travellers. At the same time one must not forget his winter landscapes of 'Aylmer, Upper Canada,' 'Orford Lake,' and 'Winter Scene on the Catterskills.' If he did, in fact, in that year make a winter trip by way of the Hudson River to Montreal and Ottawa, why are there so few sketches of winter landscapes? It is strange that Beattie says so little about Bartlett's stay in America at this time: just a brief statement about his visit at Willis' new home on the Susquehanna and the cryptic summary: 'after an absence of twelve months, Mr Bartlett recrossed the Atlantic in July' [1837] (B120). It is most unlikely that the winter scenes belong to 1838 because Beattie states that in that year Bartlett was at home 'by the end of December' (B123). It is also possible that Beattie may have been mistaken about Bartlett's 'absence of twelve months' in 1836 and 1837. Why would he not have crossed the Atlantic in the late fall, as he did in 1838, especially when Susanna must have been alone with two babies, one of whom the father may not have seen? If he did, in fact, spend the winter months with his wife, then it is much easier to explain the lack of American winter landscapes. The three that do exist may have been based, in part, upon winter scenes done by other artists and, in part, upon what he saw in November and December, 1838.

If Beattie's inability or reluctance to give more detail than he does about Bartlett's visits to America in 1836–7, 1838, and 1841 is puzzling, even more so is his disposal of Bartlett's diaries and correspondence. That Beattie had access to the letters and journals is obvious from his several references to them. As early as 1835 Bartlett was sending written accounts of his travels on to Beattie. In one of his surviving letters (6 June 1835) he says: 'I am much obliged by the care you have kindly taken of my notes – your approbation is a real encouragement.' The sixteen letters held in the Central Library at the London Borough of Camden raise interesting questions. There seems to be no particular reason why they should have been kept and other letters and journals discarded or returned to the Bartlett family. The search of wills belonging to Bartlett's descendants reveals no reference to manuscript material. It may be, of course, that Beattie deliberately disposed of the letters, diaries, and journals which he used for his *Brief Memoir*. Certainly Beattie's own literary remains indicate that they were selected so carefully that nothing of a confidential nature was left.

Bartlett's sudden death off Malta on 13 September 1854 (B141), the result probably of health so strained that it could no longer withstand the perils of disease in the Middle East, accounts very largely for the scarcity of first-hand information about him today. With five children ranging in age from six to nineteen, his widow had, in her straitened circumstances, too much to do to be closely concerned about her husband's records. As he had been absent from home so often and for long periods, much credit must go to her for encouraging her sons to secure professional and trade qualifications. The eldest, John Spencer, took his BA in 1858 and was ordained an Anglican priest in 1859. Frederick Henry, the second son, was an articled clerk solicitor in 1861; his death certificate reveals his occupation as that of solicitor. The third son, Thomas Lemon, was listed in the 1861 Census Return as a commercial clerk. Only one of the children, John Spencer, seems to have left any written record. In 1855 he published a small volume, *The History of the Christian Church*, and in 1870 another containing twenty-seven of his sermons. Neither of the girls married, and it appears that there are no descendants of the family left today.

Beattie undertook to write the biography of his friend with the idea of helping the widow and her five children. The *Brief Memoir* raised £400.0.0 In addition, Beattie prevailed upon the prime minister to grant the artist's widow a pension of £75.0.0. a year. In 1861 Susanna Bartlett was living at 9 Grove Terrace, Kentish Town. She died in 1902 at 53 Dartmouth Park Hill, Highgate.[115] Beattie's generous efforts to help the family are a tangible indication that he valued Bartlett's friendship as much as the artist had valued his own 'unvarying kindness' to him for more than twenty years.

VIII

Any critical assessment of the hundreds of sketches which Bartlett made and of the books which he wrote must be tempered somewhat by the effect which the artist's own attitude to the circumstances of his life had upon his work. Bartlett's outlook, of course, cannot be an excuse to justify the minute references which are made to his work in substantial histories of nineteenth-century English art. But his determination to provide an adequate living for his family does explain in large part why he was accustomed to 'describe himself as a machine, destined to perform a certain number of revolutions' (B136) for George Virtue's thriving publishing firm. His acceptance of numerous commissions from Virtue to which he could 'never secure any permanent share or copyright' (B142) meant, in fact, that he had to attempt too much in too little time with the result that he could make no careful evaluation of the aesthetic conventions and theories which he accepted as binding upon his art. What he was unwilling or unable to do was to take time to develop his talents as a watercolourist. Had he done so, it is reasonable to assume that he might have approached the kind of excellence which so many artists of the Norwich School possessed. It is interesting to note in this connection that in the last year of his apprenticeship Bartlett did submit watercolours for the 1829 Norwich Exhibition.[116]

How badly Bartlett ever wanted to become recognized as a watercolourist is uncertain. What is known, however, relates to Beattie's observation about his anxiety 'to maintain his wife and children in credit and respectability,' a laudable middle-class objective but one rather in the way of the sacrifice that would have been necessary to place him among the best-known watercolourists of his time.

He was very much an Englishman: Church of England, conservative, loyal to his queen and empire. Standing on the Upper Baracca in Valetta he thrilled to the sight: ' ... the *ne plus ultra* of military and naval grandeur – a mass of forts and batteries bristling with cannon, sheltering in their powerful arms an extensive harbour, studded with enormous ships of the line and steam frigates – an exhibition of power, which, associated with a sense of the great interests it protects, produces a feeling nearly allied to the sublime.'[117] At the same time he contrasted 'the clean and ruddy English soldier, and the pale and greasy Maltese priest: the former certainly the highest type of his profession; an assertion which may not be perhaps uncharitably reversed of the latter.'[118]

He was not, however, indifferent or blind to imperfections of his society or age. He disapproved of a 'jovial band' of Britain's 'grog inspired sailors ... rolling down [Valetta] steps, and sweeping all before them on the way to the harbour, with small regard to the feelings of any unfortunate natives who may happen to be in their way.'[119] On one occasion he even questioned Britain's right to one of her proudest possessions, Gibraltar. There was a need, he said, to ' ... vindicate our very equivocal right to the jurisdiction of a fortress which, if the truth must be confessed, we obtained in a very equivocal manner, and make use of for purposes more equivocal still.'[120]

Rather paradoxically, it was just because of his acceptance of the aesthetic hand-me-downs of the Romantic age and because of his willingness to look at the world as it was rather than as it should be that Bartlett prints, plain or tinted, are now so popular. Those small, picturesque brush or pencil sketches which he made as he journeyed about Asia Minor, or toiled up Swiss passes, or moved along the great rivers of Europe or America provide reliable documentary evidence of what the countries he visited were like over a century ago. The prints link the often humdrum present with the romantic past and, in Canada especially, supply one of the most important visual records of pioneer days.

That Bartlett's name today is familiar to many who would be hard put to say four or five words about William Gilpin, Alexander Cozens, John Sell Cotman, Thomas Girtin, Samuel Prout, or David Roberts is attributable not so much to the excellence of his art as to the hundreds of impressions which the engravers of the Turner school made available from their steel engravings and which, in turn, illustrated the elegant publications that came from George Virtue's press at 26 Ivy Lane, London. Virtue's ownership of *The Art-Journal*, his American branch establishment, and his shrewd business acumen ensured that thousands of volumes bearing Bartlett illustrations were sold in Britain, America, and Europe. On the continent, for example, editions of *Switzerland Illustrated* appeared in French and German (p. 215, n12) and 'met with the same flattering reception as at home.'[121] It is the prints, often tinted and framed, taken from these volumes which now appear more than a century later in antique shops of the same picturesque lands in which Bartlett himself had travelled.

Although their artistic merit is too frequently dismissed or hidden by adjectives such as 'picturesque' and 'topographic,' Bartlett sketches often possess charm and delicacy and reveal the artist's understanding of landscape: his ability to select prospects and to use light and shade with effect to enliven his scene. The Bartlett watercolours held in the Victoria and Albert Museum and by private collectors offer conclusive proof that the artist did from time to time use colour effectively. The 'Shâri' a el-Gohergiyeh in Cairo' is a good example of his later work. Another of the Egyptian scenes in colour is the 'Island of Philæ, Looking down the River Nile.'[122] These watercolours should be compared with earlier works like that in sepia of 'Thaxted Church, Essex,' the carefully toned watercolour of 'Peterborough Cathedral,' and the soft pastel 'View of Sion.' Such a comparison reveals the range of Bartlett's art from the simple monochrome treatment of the churches and cathedrals of England to the detailed colouring of geometrical patterns on the exterior of Cairo mosques.

Although Bartlett engravings are much sought after today, there has been no corresponding demand for the travel books which he wrote and illustrated and of which so many editions appeared in the mid-nineteenth century. Several of these – *Footsteps*, *Forty Days*, *Nile Boat*, and *Overland Route* – deserve to be reprinted, for Bartlett was, like his contemporary, Edward Lear, as talented an author as he was an artist. Had he had more time to revise and shape his travel narratives, Bartlett might well have written a really memorable travel book, for he knew how to bring ' ... scenery with something of daguerreotype minuteness before the eye of the reader.'[123] He could make his reader hear from the top of the Great Pyramid at dawn '... the only sound that arose from the immense expanse of the Libyan desert ... the wailing of the winds, as they contend over its dead surface, and pile it up into shapeless swells and ridges, wakening a wild and mournful music.'[124] He knew, too, how to describe places as 'utterly disappointing' as modern Athens, where the traveller can find himself 'amid a maze of paltry streets and alleys, resembling the faubourgs of some second-rate French town, hastily run up among the tottering ruins of the old Turkish houses, which were infinitely more picturesque.' It is a town, he remarks, made up of 'shabby *estaminets* and grog houses,' 'petty milliners' shops,' 'stinking repositories for olives, salt-fish, and all unutterable things'; it even has an 'English warehouse for cheese and pickles and bottled porter, kept by the inevitable Brown or Smith.'[125]

While William Beattie and other contemporaries overestimated Bartlett's contribution to art and letters,[126] the twentieth century has underrated his achievement – indeed forgotten that he was a man of letters. He himself protested – perhaps too much – that his travel books could make no claim to originality. He was not one of the learned who had enlisted in the service of antiquity. He was, as he described himself, one of ' ... a flying corps of light-armed skirmishers, who, going lightly over the ground, busy themselves chiefly with its picturesque aspect; who aim at giving lively impressions of actual sights, and at thus creating an interest which may lead the reader to a further investigation of the subject. This class of writers can, of course, even when successful in their object, claim but a very humble rank.'[127]

If by his own admission William Henry Bartlett's place in arts and letters is a humble one, it is equally certain that it is a secure one especially in America, where – ranging from Springfield, Virginia in the south to Quebec in the north, from Niagara Falls in the west to Halifax in the east – this 'light-armed skirmisher' was able to bring back in his portfolio to his English headquarters a remarkably comprehensive and faithful impression of settlement and wilderness across the seas.

References

1 For this information I am indebted to Professor Alexander H. Brodie of the University of Guelph, who examined the St Pancras Rate-books and other relevant material in the archives of the London Borough of Camden.
2 Frederick A. Bartlett
3 Nathaniel Parker Willis, *Rural Letters and Other Records of Thought at Leisure* (Auburn, Alden, Beardsley, 1854), p. 41
4 William Henry Bartlett, *Forty Days in the Desert, on the Track of the Israelites ...* 5th. ed. (London, Arthur Hall, nd), p. 151
5 William Henry Bartlett, *The Nile Boat; or Glimpses of the Land of Egypt* (London, Arthur Hall, Virtue, 1849), pp.19–20
6 William Henry Bartlett, *Walks about the City and Environs of Jerusalem*, 1st. ed. (London, George Virtue, 1844), p. 218
7 William Henry Bartlett, *Pictures from Sicily* (London, Arthur Hall, Virtue, 1853), pp. 99-105
8 Unpublished, undated letter from W.H. Bartlett to Dr William Beattie – prior to 1844
9 John Britton, 'Mr. William Henry Bartlett,' *The Art-Journal*, (1 Jan. 1855), p. 24
10 Ibid.
11 For further details of 17 Burton Street see John Britton, *The Auto-Biography* (London, the Author, 1850), part III, pp.155–60
12 Britton, 'Mr. William Henry Bartlett,' p.25
13 Ibid.
14 Ibid.
15 Britton, *The Auto-Biography*, part II, p.112
16 John Britton, *The History and Antiquities of the Metropolitan Church of Canterbury ...* (London, Nattali, 1836), p. i
17 John Britton, *The History and Antiquities of the Cathedral Church of Worcester ...* (London, Nattali, 1836), p. xxii
18 G.N. Wright, *Ireland Illustrated* (London: H. Fisher, Son, and Jackson, 1831), pp. 61–2
19 The theory and importance of the picturesque have been treated capably by such scholars as Elizabeth Manwaring, *Italian Landscape in Eighteenth Century England;* Christopher Hussey, *The Picturesque, Studies in a Point of View;* William Templeman, *The Life and Work of William Gilpin;* Walter John Hipple, Jr., *The Beautiful, the Sublime and the Picturesque in Eighteenth-Century British Aesthetic Theory;* Carl Paul Barbier, *William Gilpin;* Edward Malins, *English Landscaping and Literature, 1660–1840.*

20 See C.E. Hughes, *Early English Water-Colour*, rev. and ed. by Jonathan Mayne (London, Benn, 1950)

21 Britton, 'Mr. William Henry Bartlett,' p. 24

22 In Henry Stebbing, *The Christian in Palestine, or Scenes of Sacred History* (London, George Virtue, [1847]), pp. 72–3

23 William Beattie, *The Waldenses, or Protestant Valleys of Piedmont, Dauphiny, and the Ban de la Roche* (London, George Virtue, 1838), p. 187

24 William Beattie, *Switzerland Illustrated*, 2 vols. (London, Virtue, 1836), II, 90

25 Edmund Burke, *A Philosophical Enquiry into the Origin of our Ideas of the Sublime and Beautiful*, ed. J.T. Boulton (London, Routledge and Kegan Paul, 1958), p. 39

26 Bartlett, *Pictures from Sicily*, p. 104

27 Bartlett, *Forty Days*, p. 65

28 [William Gilpin], *An Essay upon Prints ...* 2nd. ed. (London, G. Scott, 1768), pp. 81–2

29 Kenneth Clark, *Landscape into Art* (Boston, Beacon Press, 1961), p. 53

30 Bartlett, *Pictures from Sicily*, p. 59

31 Christopher Hussey, *The Picturesque, Studies in a Point of View* (London, Frank Cass, 1967), p. 31

32 *The Watering Places of Great Britain and Fashionable Directory Illustrated with Views* (London, I.T. Hinton, 1831), p. 71

33 For an account of Lady Blessington's life at Seamore Place see Michael Sadleir, *Blessington-D'Orsay, a Masquerade* (London, Constable, 1933), pp. 146–252

34 See Thomas Roscoe, *The Tourist in Spain, Biscay, and the Castiles*, illus. by David Roberts (London, Robert Jennings, 1837)

35 Hughes, *Early English Water-Colour*, p. 90

36 Beattie, *Switzerland*, I, 3

37 Three miles distant

38 Beattie, *Switzerland*, II, 125. See also Bartlett's own account in *Sharpe's London Journal*, XII (1848), 129–30

39 Beattie, *Switzerland*, II, 97

40 W.H. Bartlett, *Walks about the City and Environs of Jerusalem*, 2nd. ed. (London, George Virtue, nd), p. 13

41 John Carne, *Syria, the Holy Land, Asia Minor etc.* 3 vols. (London, Fisher, Son, [1838]), II, 16

42 William Henry Bartlett, *Footsteps of Our Lord and His Apostles in Syria, Greece, and Italy* (London, Arthur Hall, Virtue, 1851), p. 34

43 Ibid., p. 35; see also *Brief Memoir*, p. 161

44 Carne, *Syria*, II, 65

45 Beattie, *Waldenses*, pp. 189–90

46 N.G. van Kampen, *The History and Topography of Holland and Belgium*, tr. by W.G. Fearnside (London, George Virtue, [1837]), p. iv

47 I am indebted to Mrs E.A. Collard of Montreal for permitting me to see this sketch in her home.

48 These two sketches are in the Art Gallery of Ontario.

49 Father Louis Hennepin, *A New Discovery of a Vast Country in America*, reprinted from the second London issue of 1698 by Reuben Gold Thwaites, vol. I (Chicago, A.C. McLurg, 1903), I, 54

50 George Heriot, *Travels Through the Canadas ...* (London, Richard Phillips, 1807), p. 159

51 Ibid., p. 77

52 Miss Julia Pardoe (1806–1862) had lived for two years in Turkey where she acquired a detailed knowledge of Constantinople and the surrounding country. Her many publications included several novels, histories, biographies, a volume of poetry, and travel books on Turkey, the Rhine, Paris, and Portugal.

53 Nathaniel Parker Willis, *American Scenery; or Land, Lake, and River*, 2 vols. (London, George Virtue, 1840), II, 87–8

54 Carne, *Syria*, II, 66
55 [Julia] Pardoe, *The Beauties of the Bosphorus* (London, Virtue, 1839), p. 4
56 Eric W. Morse, 'Canoe Routes of the Voyageurs, the Geography and Logistics of the Canadian Fur Trade,' *Canadian Geographical Journal*, LXIII (July 1961), 2
57 Carne, *Syria*, II, 27
58 Ibid., 66
59 Bartlett, *Walks*, 1st ed., p. 9
60 W.H. Bartlett, *Jerusalem Revisited* (London, Arthur Hall, Virtue, 1855), p. 101
61 [W.H. Bartlett], 'Editor's Writing Desk,' *Sharpe's London Journal* ... , IX (1849), 255
62 A reasonable explanation for this distortion of some physical features is that it was a recognized convention. William Gilpin offered such advice to the 'initiated': 'In the exhibition of distant mountains on paper, or canvas, unless you make them exceed their *real* or *proportional* size, they have no effect. It is inconceivable how objects lessen by distance. Examine any distance, clothed by mountains, in a camera, and you will easily see what a poor diminutive appearance the mountains make.' *Observations Relative Chiefly to Picturesque Beauty, Made in the Year 1776, on Several Parts of Great Britain; particularly the Highlands of Scotland*, 2 vols. (London, R. Blamire, 1789), I, 146–7
63 I am indebted to the National Gallery of Canada for giving me permission to study the Bartlett sketches, 'March on Lake Chaudière,' 'Wigwam in the Forest,' and 'A First Settlement.'
64 Gérard Morisset, *Peintures et tableaux*, Les Arts au Canada Français, vol. I (Quebec, Les Editions du Chevalet, 1936), pp. 133–40. See also 'La Peinture traditionnelle au Canada Français,' *L'Encyclopédie du Canada Français*, II (Ottawa, Le Circle du Livre de France, 1960), 78
65 Henry A. Beers, *Nathaniel Parker Willis*, (Boston, Houghton Mifflin, 1893), pp. 247–8
66 [Catherine Parr Traill], *The Backwoods of Canada: being the Letters from the Wife of an Emigrant Officer* ... (London, Charles Knight, 1836), pp. 112, 156
67 Willis, *American Scenery*, I, 1
68 William Beattie, *Scotland Illustrated* ... 2 vols. (London, George Virtue, 1838), II, 53
69 This work appeared first in one volume as *Finden's Views of the Ports, Harbours, and Watering Places of Great Britain, continued by W.H. Bartlett* (London, George Virtue, 1839)
70 William Beattie, *The Danube, its History, Scenery, and Topography* (London, Virtue, 1844), p. 2
71 Ibid, p. iii
72 Ibid., p. 195, n 2
73 William Beattie, *The Castles and Abbeys of England*, 2 vols. (London, Virtue, [1851]), I, 5
74 Stebbing, *Christian in Palestine*, pp. 46–8
75 Ibid., pp. 47–8
76 Bartlett, *Walks*, 1st ed., Preface
77 Ibid., 2nd ed., Preface
78 Ibid., p. 62
79 Ibid., p. 14
80 Lamartine, *Voyage en Orient*, ed. Lotfy Fam (Paris, Librairie Nizet, nd), p. 363
81 Bartlett, *Walks*, 2nd ed., p. 100
82 Bartlett, *Footsteps*, p. 164
83 Ibid., p. 3
84 John Ruskin, too, felt on occasion 'how many suffering persons must pay for [his] picturesque subject and happy walk.' *Modern Painters* (2nd ed.; London, George Allen, 1900), IV, 10–11 n
85 Bartlett, *Jerusalem Revisited*, p. 61
86 Ibid., p. 35
87 Bartlett, *Forty Days*, p. iv
88 Ibid., p. 5
89 Ibid., p. 29

90 Ibid., p. 31

91 Bartlett, *The Nile Boat*, p. 70. See also *Forty Days*, p. 5

92 Bartlett, *Nile Boat*, p. 22

93 Ibid., p. 39

94 Ibid., pp. 134-5

95 [Bartlett], *Sharpe's London Journal*, XI (1850), Preface

96 Ibid., X (1849), 257

97 [Bartlett], 'A Night and Day in Venice,' ibid., XI (1850), 109-10

98 [W.H. Bartlett], *The Wilkie Gallery with Biographical and Critical Notices* (London & New York, George Virtue, nd), p. 5

99 Ibid., p. 35

100 It is in this chapter that Bartlett reveals the extent of his journeys in the track of St Paul: 'I had traced [St Paul's] footsteps from Jerusalem ... to Damascus ... and thence to Antioch ... I had followed his devious mission-ary course to the shores of Crete and Cyprus, and the coasts of Asia Minor, through the beautiful islands of the Archipelago, to Athens, to Corinth, and to Italy; often sailing, with the New Testament in hand, upon the very same track, looking upon the same headlands, passing through the same straits, threading the same passes, and travelling over the same highways,' pp. 86-7.

101 W.H. Bartlett, *Gleanings, Pictorial and Antiquarian, on the Overland Route* (London, Hall, Virtue, 1851), p. 210

102 Ibid., pp. 229-30

103 Bartlett, *Pictures from Sicily*, pp. 189-90

104 Ibid., p. 41

105 W.H. Bartlett, *The Pilgrim Fathers; or, The Founders of New England in the Reign of James the First* (London, Arthur Hall, Virtue, 1853), p. x

106 Ibid., p. 51

107 The Mansion House, Plymouth

108 Bartlett, *Pilgrim Fathers*, p. 164

109 Ibid., p. 194

110 This folio was acquired in 1968 by the library of the University of Guelph, Guelph, Ontario, Canada.

111 A copy of this *Catalogue* is in the British Museum (S.C. Southgate, vol. 87, т8) under the title: *A Catalogue of Water Colour Drawings, by W.H. Bartlett Esq.*

112 Edward Lear, *Journals of a Landscape Painter in Southern Calabria etc.* (London, Richard Bentley, 1852), pp. 2-3

113 W.H. Bartlett and B.B. Woodward, *The History of the United States of America*, 3 vols. (London, George Virtue, 1856), I, 503. Part of this work was published in 1852. See reference *Brief Memoir*, pp. 144-5

114 Bartlett, *History of the United States*, I, 268. See also W.H. Bartlett, 'Quebec' in *Sharpe's London Journal*, VIII (1848-9), 1-6

115 Beattie's papers contain this reference in his handwriting: 'Her Majesty has most graciously responded to the "Memorial" presented by Dr. Beattie, in favour of Mrs. S. Bartlett – widow of the distinguished artist and traveller – by granting her a pension of £75 per annum.'

116 Derek Clifford, *Watercolours of The Norwich School* (London, Cory, Adams and Mackay, 1965), p. 85

117 Bartlett, *Overland Route*, p. 22

118 Ibid., p. 8

119 Ibid., pp. 8-9

120 Ibid., pp. 204-5

121 Beattie, *Switzerland*, 'To the Reader'

122 For a reproduction of this water colour see Martin Hardie, *Water-Colour Painting in Britain*; III: *The Victorian Period* (London Batsford, 1968), plate 41.

123 Bartlett, *Footsteps*, p. 163

124 Bartlett, *Nile Boat*, p. 97

125 Bartlett, *Footsteps*, p. 101

126 *Bentley's Miscellany* offers interesting il-lustrations of how highly Bartlett was

regarded by many contemporary reviewers. Of
The Nile Boat: '... in the very first class of
illustrated travels ... furnishing us with so
much really valuable information of the most
remarkable and interesting country on the
earth ... ,' XXVII (1850), 99. Of *Footsteps*:
'... easy, unaffected, and vivacious style of
writing ... graceful and finished pictures ...

sunny splendour and serene beauty in ...
vignette views,' XXXI (1852), 15. Of *Pictures
from Sicily*: '... objective rather than sub-
jective ... charming vignette illustrations ...
Mr. Bartlett is one of the best word-painters
whom we know,' XXXIII (1853).

127 Bartlett, *Nile Boat*, p. iii

21 Gallery of the 'Tete Noire,' near Trient *sepia wash*

22 Hallowell *steel engraving*

23 Manningtree, Essex *steel engraving*

24 Faneuil Hall, Boston *steel engraving*

25 The Village of Grindelwald *steel engraving*

26 The Four Courts, Dublin *steel engraving*

27 The Twa Brigs of Ayr *steel engraving*

28 Village of Little Falls *steel engraving*

29 Glengarriff *steel engraving*

30 Constantinople, from Scutari *sepia wash*

31 Constantinople, from Scutari *steel engraving*

32 Well at Catania *sepia wash*

33 A Nunnery in Palermo *sepia wash*

34 The Grass Market, Edinburgh *steel engraving*

35 Town Hall, Boston *sepia wash*

36 Leyden and the Old Rhine from the Spaniard's Bridge *sepia wash*

BRIEF MEMOIR

OF THE LATE

William Henry Bartlett

Author of

Walks about Jerusalem;
Forty Days in the Desert;
The Nile-Boat;
The Footsteps of Our Lord and His Apostles;
The Pilgrim Fathers;
Jerusalem Revisited;
and other works

BY WILLIAM BEATTIE MD

Author of

Switzerland Illustrated,
Life of Thomas Campbell,
etc, etc.

PUBLISHED BY SUBSCRIPTION

LONDON

PRINTED BY M.S. RICKERBY, 73 CANNON STREET, CITY

MDCCCLV

LONDON

MARY S. RICKERBY, PRINTER, CANNON STREET, CITY

Subscribers

	Copies		Copies
The Right Rev. the Lord Bishop of London	5	S. Bellin, Esq, Camden Street	2
Mrs Blomfield	1	Mrs Berthoud, Higher Broughton	1
The Right Hon. Sir F.G. Moon, Bart., Lord Mayor of London	5	John Blakston, Esq, H.M. Customs	1
The Right Hon. the Lord Chief Baron Pollock	2	R.C. Bloomfield, Esq	1
		John W.F. Blundell, Esq, MD, 32 Finsbury Circus	1
Sir Samuel Morton Peto, Bart.	1	Joseph Bonomi, Esq	1
Sir George Hayter	2	W.J. Booth, Esq, Red Lion Square	1
		Mrs Borely, Ombersley	1
Mrs Adie, Lichfield	1	E. Brandard, Esq, Albion Grove East, Islington	1
R.B. Allen, Esq, Walthamstow	1	Samuel Briggs, Esq	1
Rev. M.J. Anderson, Pendleton, Manchester	1	E. Bristow, Esq, Clapham Park	1
Samuel Angell, Esq, 18 Gower Street	1	John Britton, Esq, FSA	1
Alfred Ashton, Esq, 8 St Paul's Road, Camden Town	1	Henry G. Brown, Esq, Higham Hill, Walthamstow	5
		Joseph Browne, Esq, Aberdeen Lodge, Brighton	1
Mrs Baggallay, St Thomas's Hospital	1	Miss Buff, Rockferry, Cheshire	1
R. Baggallay, Esq, Clapham	2	D. Burton, Esq, Spring Gardens	1
G. Bagster, Esq	1	Mrs C. Busk, Maize Hill, Greenwich	1
Miss Bancroft, Hyde Park Terrace	1		
W. Beamont, Esq, Warrington	1	Alfred Catherwood, Esq, MD, Charles Square, Hoxton	1
Rev. W.J. Beamont	1	F.A. Catherwood, Esq	1
Wm. Beattie, Esq, MD, Tavistock Street, Bedford Square	10	Thos. Chatteris, Esq, Upper Clapton	1

	Copies		Copies
Mrs Roylance Child, Tavistock Street, Bedford Square	2	S. Griffin, Esq, Portsea	1
Miss Clapton	1	Hudson Gurney, Esq, FRS	3
Rhodes Cobb, Esq, Twickenham, and Friends	6	George Gutch, Esq, Porteus House	1
Mrs E. Coleman, Sumner Place, Brompton	1	S.C. Hall, Esq, FSA	1
Mrs John Cooke, Upper Vernon St.	1	Charles Hanbury, Esq	5
A.A. Crole, Esq, Finsbury Circus	1	N.E.S.A. Hamilton, Esq, Finchley	1
Rev. John Cumming, DD	1	Wm. C. Harding, Esq, Thame, Oxon	1
William Curling, Esq, Denmark Hill	2	Rev. Dr Harris, President of New College, St John's Wood	2
Joseph Curling, Esq, Herne Hill	1	Mrs Hornby, Winwick Hall, Lancash.	5
		W. Hosking, Esq, Woburn Square	1
John Davies, Esq, Round Hill, Sydenham	2	Owen Jones, Esq, 9 Argyll Place	3
Mrs John Davies, Sen., Brighton	1	E. Joynson, Esq, Effingham Lodge, St Mary Crag	1
James Davies, Esq, Croydon	1	W. Joynson, Esq, Rookery, St Mary Crag	1
Rev. N. Davis, FRS, SA, 14 Brunswick Square	1		
Mrs R. Dawson, Moselle Villa, Tottenham	1	Miss Keating and Miss Davies, Bruce House, Tottenham	1
Mrs Chas. Denham, Lansdowne Villa	1	Rev. R.B. Kennard, MA	1
T.L. Donaldson, Professor of Architecture, London University	1	Miss Kilvington	1
W.L. Donaldson, Esq, 18 Southampton Street	1	H. King, Esq, 239 Up. Thames Street	5
		G.G. Kirby, Esq, Great Cumberland Place	2
P. Fish, Esq, Highbury Terrace	1	Hen. C. Lacy, Esq, Richmond, Surrey	5
Miss Fleming, Cookham Grove	1	Mrs Lewis Lacy, Aberdeen	1
Charles Fowler, Esq, Fairseat, near Wrotham	1	G.H. Ladbury, Esq, Elm Lodge, Upper Holloway	1
Alexander Fraser, Esq, Truman's Brewery, Spitalfields	1	Jas. Laming, Esq, Maida Hill, West	5
Rev. T.M. Fraser, Gifford, Scotland	1	James Laming, Jun., Esq	2
		Richard Laming, Esq	1
		Frederick Lawrence, Esq	1
G. Gambert, Esq, Hornsey	1	Miss Lemon, Upp. Porchester Street, Hyde Park	2
Miss Gasse, St Albans	1	Charles Leslie, Esq, RA	1
Ralph Gilbert, Esq, Sydenham	1	Benjamin Luppet, Esq	1
J.H. Good, Jun., Esq, 75 Hatton Garden	1		
John Griffith, Esq, 16 Finsbury Place South	1	Mrs Mackinlay, Lansdowne Place, Brighton	1

	Copies		Copies
W. McDonough, Esq, Bank of England	1	James Ridgeway, Esq, 32 Victoria Road, Kensington	1
Miss McMahon, Blomfield Crescent	1	F. Rivington, Esq	1
Miss Manning	2	David Roberts, Esq, RA	1
Frederick Marriott, Esq, 9 Regent's Park Terrace, Gloucester Gate	1	Miss Robinson, Cumberland Street	1
J.J. Masquerier, Esq, Brighton	2	Samuel Rogers, Esq, FRS, St James's Place	1
Robert Miller, Esq, Grove Hill	1	Miss Martha Rogers	1
D. Mocatta, Esq, 57 Old Broad Street	1	Thomas Roscoe, Esq	1
James Moon, Esq, Milman Street	1	G.C. Russell, Esq, Camden Square	1
A.G. Moon, Esq	1		
F. Moon, Esq, Milman Street	1	Thomas Sawyer, Esq, Ramsgate	1
David Moore, Esq, Kensington	1	Captain Sawyer, Southampton	1
Mrs Morison, Mornington Road, Regent's Park	10	Miss M. Sayer, 28 Upper Seymour Street	1
J.C. Morison, Esq	10	Charles Seipelt, Esq, Liverpool	1
		Edw. Sharman, Esq, Wellingborough	1
Dr Neale, Ombersley	1	Samuel Sharpe, Esq, and Family, Highbury Terrace	10
Mrs Neale, 2 St George's Terrace, Islington	1	Rev. Philip Smith, BA, Head Master of Mill Hill School	1
Mrs Needham, Palace Gardens	1	Henry Smith, Esq, 33 Chalcot Villas, Haverstock Hill	1
Lewis Newnham, Esq, MD, Camberwell	1	H.H. Smith, Esq, Admiralty, Somerset House	1
John B. Nichols, Esq	1	Job Smith, Esq, Hornsey	1
		Thomas Spalding, Esq, Hendon	1
S. Olding, Esq	2	Clarkson Stanfield, Esq, RA	1
– Ostler, Esq	1	Rev. Arthur Penryn Stanley	5
Mrs Owen, Goppa, Denbigh	1	Rev. Henry Stebbing, DD, FRS	1
W. Owen, Esq, Tan-y-gyrt, Denbigh	1	Lieut.-Colonel Strode, The Cedars, Ombersley	1
R.M. Phipson, Esq, Ipswich	1	Edward Taverner, Esq, Stoke Newington	3
Mrs Phipson, Thames Street	1	Mrs Taylor, Forest Hill	1
H. Pidcock, Esq, Woodfield, Ombersley	1	– Thaine, Esq	1
Mrs Poignard, Westbourne Terrace	1	Seth Thompson, Esq, MD, Lower Seymour Street	1
J. Powell, Esq, Hamilton Terrace	1	Charles Tilt, Esq, Hendon	1
James Powell, Esq, The Limes, Upper Clapton	1	J.B. Tippetts, Esq, Lonsdale Square	1
John Procter, Esq	1		
Joseph Procter, Esq, 18 Cheapside	1		
Miss Rickerby	1		

	Copies		Copies
Wm Tipping, Esq, Seven Oaks	1	W. Wallop, Esq, 2 Kensington Gate	1
Mrs Frederick O. Thompson,		R. Warton, Esq, Finchley	1
Hyde Park Place	1	William Williams, Esq, Rood Lane	1
Mrs Toms and Miss Lolley,		George Williams, Esq, Clifton Villas	1
Grove Road, Brixton	1	Mrs Williams	1
Rev. H. Townley, Highbury Place	1	A. Wilmore, Esq, Regent Square	1
John Turner, Esq, Wilton Street	1	Miss Wilson, Tunbridge Wells	1
		William Woodburn, Esq, The Lawn,	
C.J. Venables, Esq	1	Haverstock Hill	2
Samuel Vessey, Esq, Halton Manor,		C. Woodward, Esq, FRS,	
Spilsby, Lincolnshire	1	10 Compton Terrace	1
Miss Vessey	1	The Rev. T.P. Wright, Hackney	1
J.H. Vessey, Esq	1	J.H. Wyatt, Esq	1

94

A Brief Memoir
of
William Henry Bartlett

William Henry Bartlett was born at Kentish Town, near London, on the 26th of March, 1809. He was the second child of his parents; and under the care of an excellent mother – whose loss he afterwards so keenly felt and deplored – he discovered, even in infancy, those rudiments of genius which it was her delightful task to foster and mature. She lived long enough to reap the fruits of her maternal vigilance; for having committed the seeds of parental instruction to a healthy and grateful soil, it amply repaid the culture and realized the expectations which she had so fondly indulged. His physical powers were never robust; he was an apt, delicate, and sensitive child, but with a natural turn for reading and reflection, his mind rapidly expanded. About the age of seven, or little more, he was placed under the discipline of a boarding-school in the neighbourhood; and there, as he has told us, he entered into a little world at variance with all his childish sympathies and predilections. This was an event which threw a cloud over the morning of his life, and enters into many of his retrospective notes. And here I may premise, that, as the period under notice is very little known to his surviving friends, I consider it my duty to lay before them more extracts from his private memoranda than will be necessary at a later period, when his published works became at once the index and repository of his thoughts and occupations. In allusion to his first quitting the parental hearth, he writes:

'Even now I recollect the agony of my grief at the idea of being sent to a boarding-school; the sinking of heart, the feeling of utter isolation, and abandonment, with which I first found myself immured within its walls. The measure had been dictated by the kindest motives, but the influence it had in promoting a morbid sensitiveness of character was deplorable.

'From being petted and indulged at home, I was suddenly transported amidst a crowd of lads, almost all older than myself, by whom I was cuffed and buffeted about, with all that petty tyranny which boys often love to exercise towards those weaker than themselves. But the bitterest thing was the total deprivation of affectionate intercourse with my parents, and the feeling of having no one, in the multitude around, who loved or cared for me. I was thus thrown inwardly upon myself; my natural feeling of affection, hitherto so freely exercised, found no vent, and I became sad, self-concentrated, and morbidly sensitive.

'The years I spent at school present a dreary monotony: but in justice to similar institutions, I am bound to say that, both as regards the comfort and the education of the pupils, this school was very badly conducted. To a child of a naturally sensitive temperament, it furnished nothing but the worst of training. The bold alone, the cunning, the selfish, and the harsh, indulged and fostered their evil qualities in its unwholesome soil. The system of tuition was wretched: no emulation was enkindled to induce the love of learning; but the practice of flogging – unjustly and absurdly inflicted at the caprice of the master – tended to brutalize the feelings, and produce a positive disgust for study.

'As to any attempt to form the mind, there was none: it was left to its natural or rather unnatural growth. The ardent faculties of youth, just bursting forth, seized for their nutriment whatever could be met with. Imagination dwelt with rapture on visions of romance, wherever they were brought within its grasp, or invented them, when wanting. Never shall I forget the feelings with which myself and other boys devoured the pages of Miss Porter's *Scottish Chiefs*, and the struggle there was to get hold of it, even for half an hour. It was a little world of beings of the mind, suddenly opened to us – an oasis in the dreary desert of school-life – the vividness of which can only be painted by the memory of others, if haply they have experienced the same. Any little event which occurred within our walls was magnified, and coloured with the hues of wonder.' In illustration of this he mentions, 'the adventures of three parlour-boarders, who, in consequence of being flogged, made their escape from school, and, in spite of all pursuit, arrived safe in the north of England. In those days, when railroads were not even dreamed of, these enterprising comrades were looked upon as superior beings. Thus, the various propensities of nature were gradually developed – affording a mimic, but too faithful image of the future man. And such – though but faintly depicted – were the depressing influences under which the years of boyhood were passed.'

This melancholy picture is somewhat relieved by the following passage: 'But kindly nature, not to be wholly repressed though cruelly outraged, often visited my heart with her sweet and consolatory stirrings, and kept alive her sacred fire in its deep recess. The self-concentration to which I was reduced, prepared for me that mood of mind, which has been the main consolation of my life, and the great antagonist of my baser qualities – the love of the eternal beauty of the Universe, the harmony of which I already began to perceive, and to feel my heart thrilled with a secret rapture. Return, if only for a brief moment – return, ye rosy hours of unchecked and joyous impulse, with which my sad school days were not unfrequently chequered! Return, ye gay holidays spent in the open fields – in green places under the shadow of the perfumed lime-trees; or the bright flowers, and broad green rustling fans of the horse-chestnuts! I can still see the stile where, on half-holidays, I was accustomed to sit, with my younger brother, who came up to see me, with a little store of sweetmeats. And well do I remember the quiet afternoon, which, once a month, I spent at home – a few hours of "fearful joy"* snatched by my mother's side. And then her little treat of tea and cake; the walk back with her to the school; and the choking sensation with which I received her parting kiss.'

Thus, with little pleasure, and still less improvement, his school days drew to a close. 'At the age of twelve,' he writes, 'I returned home; and it became an object of great anxiety to my mother to place me out in life.' Various plans were suggested by friends who had experience in directing the pursuits of youth – some recommending a learned profession, others a trade, which might lead to competence, without the mortifications and disappointments which too often beset the path of more ambitious aspirants. But, for what appeared sound reasons at the time, the youth was encouraged to look to another source for preferment; and, having from infancy, evinced a taste for the fine arts, it was thought more prudent to consult the natural bias, than to force his thoughts into a channel so foreign to his preconceived notions and predilections. In after life, however, like a late distinguished writer, he often expressed his regret that he

* 'And snatched a fearful joy' – Gray.

had not been apprenticed to some unambitious trade, in which the labour of the hand might have lightened that of head and heart. This, however, was but the regret, too general among men, and well expressed by the poet Campbell.

With other touching reminiscences of his schoolboy experience narrated with unaffected simplicity, the period arrived when he commenced the first labours of a profession, which was to give him high and lasting distinction among contemporary artists. This, however, could not be accomplished at once: a kind, intelligent master was to be found; and as the choice was an affair of no little moment – difficulties soon presented themselves which at first sight had been overlooked; and, while arrangements were pending, young Bartlett was taken from school, and for a season resumed his place at the family hearth. The holidays that followed were enhanced by recollections of the harsh discipline and restraint from which he had just escaped. The intervals were filled up with delicious rambles among shady groves, 'spring-green lanes,' and undulating pastures; while every successive ramble implanted in his heart a deeper love of nature, and gave him a more and more decided taste for the picturesque in landscape.

At this period he writes: 'My delight was in solitary walks about the green neighbourhood of my native suburb, either early in the morning, or more frequently in the evening. Here I revelled in the growing luxury of a deep sense of the harmonies which nature unfolds to her true votaries. The rich hues of sunset, the melodies of rustling groves, the solemnity of twilight, and the starry heavens, I drank in with silent enthusiasm. These things were to me inward nourishment; they opened to me, as it were, a new world into which I retired from certain harsh and cruel circumstances, which would otherwise have broken my spirit.'

An eligible occasion having now presented itself, young Bartlett was articled as apprentice to Mr Britton for seven years; and, with several other youths of talent and promise, took possession of the vacant place in his establishment, which had already attained the highest reputation as a school of architectural drawing.

The meritorious labours of Mr Britton require neither support nor eulogy in this place; they are known and appreciated by every man of taste; and in that department, to which he has devoted a long and honourable life, he stands alone as an ardent and successful reviver of the fine arts. It was in his studio, and under his tuition, that some of the most eminent and successful artists of the day made their first start on the road to fame. From that studio also where, at a patriarchal age, he still cultivates the muses – an autobiography has just issued, which happily combines a fund of anecdote, information, and amusement, which nothing but long and varied experience could furnish.

In a late notice of his lamented pupil [*Art-Journal*, January 1855], Mr Britton thus commemorates the event in question: 'Mr Bartlett was articled to me for seven years, in 1822, and subsequently had many opportunities of sketching and drawing from nature and art, not only from the best specimens by Hearne, Alexander, Cotman, Girtin, and Turner, but from several noted ruins in Wiltshire, Somersetshire, Yorkshire, and other districts; also from the splendid and marvellous Cathedrals of those counties, and the picturesque scenery with which some of the edifices are connected. When pleased with a subject, he manifested such avidity and powers of pencilling that he made rapid progress in the art he wooed, and afterwards won. Bartlett was the fourth pupil I had taken: for these I built a comfortable and pleasant office, in the midst of a garden – a rarity in London – and provided them with all necessary materials, and also numerous books, drawings, prints, and sketches, for study. In the course of one year, Bartlett surpassed all his associates and rivals in accuracy, style, and rapidity, though others had been practising more than double his time. I soon found that he was eager to study and dwell upon the better class of works placed before him; and was particularly inquisitive about maps, travels, voyages, geography, and even Paterson's and other Road-books.'

In the statement of these interesting facts, the predilections of the young artist are clearly indicated. In his early partiality for travels and voyages, as manifested in Mr Britton's studio, the taste and talent for enterprise, which afterwards impelled him to visit the classic and remote scenes of antiquity, and transmit to after times the fruits of his masterly pencil, are distinctly foreshadowed. Here 'the boy was father to the man': the subjects which fascinated his mind and imagination at fourteen, had lost nothing of their charm at forty; but what in youth he had only indulged and longed for, assumed a more and more tangible form as he advanced in his career; until at last, through many dangers and difficulties, the ardent dreams of his boyhood were realized in a thousand beautiful forms.

Reverting to the progress of his favourite pupil, Mr Britton continues: 'To sketch and study from nature, I sent him successively into Essex, Kent, Bedfordshire, Wiltshire, and other parts of England. Following the footsteps, and studying some of the buildings and scenes, which had been previously sketched by Prout, Cotman, and Mackenzie, his progress kept pace with his enthusiasm. After the second and third year's diligent study and practice, he was occupied for some weeks on the romantic scenery around Dorking – particularly in making finished drawings of landscape, including the mansion of Deepdene, the classic seat of Thomas Hope, Esq, author of *Anastasius*.

'As Mr Bartlett advanced in age, and in artistic qualifications, he was successively engaged in studying the countless beauties, and architectural peculiarities of the cathedral churches of Bristol, Gloucester, and Hereford; from which he executed a series of elaborate drawings for my *Cathedral Antiquities of England*.'[1] These buildings afforded him subjects and matter for study – not merely as illustrations of the fine, original architecture of the middle ages, but for picturesque and scenic effects; for variety and beauty in the countless forms and details, to be found in each of those buildings; and likewise in the novelties and variations of each single edifice, as contra-distinguished from all the others. Hence they constitute a school of Art, to the architectural student, and general antiquary; and Bartlett found them of infinite value to him in after life.

In his retrospective notes, Mr Bartlett thus commemorates the pleasing excitement by which he was animated in these absorbing studies: 'I remember, with delight, my first journeys to venerable buildings, in the neighbourhood of the Metropolis, and with what mingled awe and antiquarian curiosity I surveyed them. This feeling grew with my growth; and, at a later period, tinged with the love of nature and poetry, it became a source of exquisite enjoyment. As my services became useful, I was often sent on expeditions to distant parts of England, where the beauties of nature were most conspicuous, or the gorgeous monuments of antiquity most abundant. With what deep interest have I wandered over the breezy downs of Wiltshire, in search of memorials of the Druidical, Danish, and early British times: the gray, lone cromlech, in its grassy dell, crusted over with the yellow lichens of centuries; the green monumental mounds or barrows, which enclose the ashes of the hardy warriors of those stirring times, or the more awful circles of Stonehenge and Avebury. In remote villages, too, I sought out the Saxon church, rude and simple in form, and the lofty towers and sky-pointing spires of a later age.

'Our Cathedrals are a world in themselves! In my pilgrim visits, I was accustomed to sit whole days in their solemn aisles, entranced with the rolling thunder of the organ through their lofty arches, and the chant of the matin and vesper hymns, as they died slowly away, with soul-like tenderness, among their time-worn intricacies of tombs and shrines!'

This fine passage might suffice – were other proofs wanting – to show how richly the mind of the young artist was imbued with the purest elements of poetry; and how unconsciously his language refines and softens into melody whenever he approaches those hallowed shrines, and gives vent to the associations with which his heart was filled. At a later period, when called upon to embody his descriptions in prose, and so write himself down to the popular standard, he made an effort to prune whatever savoured of poetical style and sentiment. But he could never subdue the natural impulse which guided his taste; and few readers, it may be presumed, will regret that, in his pen-and-pencil sketches, there is a happy union of poetry and prose by which they are mutually enhanced and relieved.

'In visiting several of our English cities, our young and accomplished artist was tempted by the fascinating forms, details, and scenic grouping of architecture, with rock, wood, and water, with their picturesque accompaniments, to make sketches and drawings of castles, bridges, old houses, bays, ruined gateways, etc., which induced me to undertake the publication of a large quarto volume, entitled, *Picturesque Antiquities of English Cities.*'[2] The merit of this work – by far the most elaborately finished of all Mr Britton's pictorial series – is candidly attributed to Mr Bartlett; and down to the present time, it is still without a rival.

In the summer of 1829, while his apprenticeship was drawing to a close, Mr Bartlett spent 'several weeks amidst the monastic ruins of Yorkshire, and produced a series of coloured drawings, which not only astonished his friends, but excited the admiration of some of the best draughtsmen of the time. They are devoid of the mannerism which almost all artists, young or old, exhibit in their studies and drawings of ancient buildings and scenery combined. Bartlett's subjects are drawn with admirable accuracy of line and form, particularly those of Fountains, Roche, Rivaulx, and other abbeys, with their rich accompaniments of picturesque scenery. Original in style and colouring, they faithfully portray both the architecture and the landscape of every individual scene, and are not deteriorated by imitation of any popular or fashionable artist. Hence they may

101

be referred to as the foundation of Bartlett's style – his powers of mind and hand, as progressively employed and displayed in the multitude of his topographical works.'

In a letter to his venerable master, written only five years ago, Mr Bartlett thus adverts to their joint labours in search of the picturesque: 'I have a vivid recollection of the first awakening of the antiquarian spirit within me under your tuition: of drives and walks about the Wiltshire Downs, of the great gig-umbrella, swaying to and fro, as we jolted along to the danger of being all capsized. I have visions of cromlechs, stone temples, old churches, and crumbling gateways, with a host of other and minor objects. But, alas! succeeding impressions have so huddled them together, that whenever I try to fix on details, and specific objects, and facts, all vanish into thin air and misty generalization.' And no wonder, for his mind was so filled with scenes on the Bosphorus, the Nile, and the Desert, that he might well be excused if those of Wiltshire had lost somewhat of their original freshness.

To the character and talents of Mr Britton, his grateful pupil has paid the following tribute: 'My master was a man who had raised himself by sheer talent and force of character. Of a naturally quick mind, nothing could quench its activity. His spare moments were devoted to literature, and the original bias of his mind leading him to antiquarian pursuits, his perseverance surmounted and almost supplied the defects of education. With indefatigable activity, self-confidence, never at fault, and assisted by others whose labours he had the tact to direct wisely, the works he produced formed an era in illustrated literature, and gave a wide and powerful impulse to the study and revival of Gothic architecture. But the "profoundly learned," who were not equally successful in giving it a popular shape, were rather bitter in their criticisms. But their sentence was the unjust verdict of envy whenever it was applied to his best works. By these, and the general reputation they have procured him, he enjoyed what might be called an enviable position. There was much in his occupations that tended to elevate the mind, and communicate an elegant taste. He lived in an atmosphere of antiquity. His library was crusted with the venerable folios of Camden and his followers, whose busts and portraits adorned his shelves. Models of Druidical remains, fragments of Gothic carving from churches and cathedrals, drawings of the various styles of our domestic architecture everywhere met the eye, and awakened curiosity. Thus, it was impossible but that some portion of the master's spirit should descend to his pupils.' In a later paper he [W.H. Bartlett] writes: 'Among those who have done much – more perhaps than is generally believed or admitted – towards the diffusion of a general taste for the study and investigation of English antiquities, and for their careful preservation also, we may unhesitatingly distinguish the literary veteran, John Britton, whose auto-biography is now before the public.'*

The term of his apprenticeship having expired, Mr Bartlett became a journey-man in the profession – a candidate for employment, which was all that, in the estimation of competent judges, he required to insure the united rewards of fame and competence. To his own mind, however, the promise seemed of tardy fulfilment; for, at the early age of twenty-one he moralizes, with some despon-dency, on the irksomeness of his position and the uncertainty of his prospects. How many distinguished artists, conscious of their own powers, but chilled by neglect and discouragements, have pined under similar disappointments, each waiting for the hour and occasion that should call him to the free exercise of his talents, and smooth the way to honourable distinction! The following are his reflections: 'Thus, through accidental circumstances, does the natural tempera-ment come to receive that mould which it must retain through life. Had the sagacious counsel I have alluded to† been followed, and, instead of seeking the means of subsistence by a genteel but precarious avocation, I had been drilled into the routine of some steady trade, probably a large proportion of my cares in after life had been spared me. My interests and associations had then been all local and confined. Beyond parish squabbles, and the cares or rivalry of business, the morbid effervescence of my temperament would have found its only vent in national politics, or the excitement of some narrow form of religion; whilst the sense of universal beauty – that glorious but troublesome instinct, to which the higher pains and pleasures of life are connected – like some tree in a narrow court, amidst the crowded buildings and foul air of a city, unable to put forth its foliage – would have maintained a struggling and stunted existence, starved down to the wholesome point of *nil admirari*: the great art of contentedness.

'But,' he continues, 'whatever may have been the sufferings prepared for one of sensitive and morbid temperament, naturally unfitted for struggling with the world – by the uncertain career thus opening before me, it was exactly suited for the development of my peculiar qualities of mind, and required only a better mode of elementary instruction, perhaps, to have constituted my best path in

* *Sharpe's Magazine* – Edited by W.H. Bartlett.   † A trade as already mentioned.

life .... ' Again : 'Familiarity with the privations of others, nourished a thoughtful and melancholy temperament, but greatly weakened the force of the active powers. An early cloud had been cast over my existence, and life was not with me an object of sanguine pursuit. I was, in a manner, shut out from society; and I was conscious of wanting that cheerful and ready spirit which gives a charm to social intercourse. For indifference to dress, and manners, and unconquerable shyness, I was often complained of by my master, who knew the marketable value of superficial accomplishments. But it was in vain. I had no impulse, and could not rise above the cloud of morbid depression which early suffering had produced. With me, in fact, both the pains and pleasures of life were inward and unseen. The higher faculties of the mind were now unfolding; and, with blind and passionate eagerness, laying hold of whatever could afford them scope and nourishment.

'My education had been wretched in the extreme – consisting merely of an imperfect knowledge of Latin, French, arithmetic, and such miscellaneous information on general subjects as I had picked up rather by my own reading than any formal instruction.* Of sciences I had no idea; no course of instruction on such subjects, as are now deemed almost indispensable, had been given with my miserable smattering of school learning. I had been wasting some years under a bad system.

'In the mean time,' he concludes, 'accidental circumstances added to my enjoyments. Part of my mother's house was occupied by the widow of a poet,[3] whose untimely death had left her alone in the world, and in the height of youth and beauty. Absorbed in the memory of her husband and his pursuits, the pale intellectual beauty of her noble countenance, the seclusion of her habits, and the amiability of her manners, caused me to look up to her with a feeling allied to veneration. It happened that she was absent for a length of time in the country, and at that precise period I was seized with a fever, from which my recovery was long and tedious. For greater quiet I was allowed to occupy her rooms, and made welcome to the treasures of her library, which contained what, to me, was a world of feeling which had too much affinity with my own, though rude and uncultivated. In the poems of Byron, Keats, and others, I found that my own love of nature was reflected as into the softer and more harmonious mirror of a

* In after life, by close study and application, Mr Bartlett became remarkable for the variety and extent of his information.

lake, imbued with a thousand high and affecting associations. It was then I first read of Italy and its romantic wonders – its glorious antiquities and cities, and the indescribable poetry of its climate and scenery.'

His prospects, however, began to brighten: he had now offers of employment, which, if not liberal, were likely to be permanent, and, to a certain extent, remunerative. Whatever had come from his pencil in contributions to Mr Britton's illustrations, had its full market value, as well as its meed of admiration with the public. Thus encouraged, he resolved to make a strong effort on his own account; and, although he could not 'command success,' he would do more – he would deserve it.

Observing the same studious and retired habits, so often mentioned in his private notes, he mixed very little in general society. His pleasures were confined to reading, to frequent excursions in the provinces, and to the conversation of one or two friends, whose tastes and feelings were in harmony with his own. These habits, early indulged, continued to grow upon him. Accustomed to associate with Nature in her most solitary haunts – to study the monuments of Art in all their grandeur and decay – he became silent and contemplative; and the chief happiness to which he looked forward was that which is to be found at the domestic hearth. Under these circumstances he paid his addresses to Miss Susanna Moon, niece of the present Lord Mayor; and on July 6, 1831, he was happily united to the 'wife of his choice.'

Shortly after their marriage, Mr and Mrs Henry Bartlett proceeded on a visit to a relation in Holland, where they spent a month. During this time Mr Bartlett made an excursion of ten days up the Rhine, the first and happiest of that long series of travels with which his name is so honourably identified. On their return to London he fixed his residence in his native suburb. Here he resumed his connexion with the publisher, in whose employment, as artist, author, and editor, he spent the residue of his short, but exemplary and laborious life.

SWITZERLAND ILLUSTRATED

My first interview with Mr Bartlett was in the spring of 1832. He was introduced to me by Mr Henry Jorden, who spoke of his friend in terms of well-merited commendation. I was then bringing out a small work,* with two or three views

* *Journal of Three Summers at the Minor Courts, etc.* Dedicated to the late King.

in Upper Saxony, sketched on the spot, but which the pencil of an artist was required to prepare for the engraver. Whilst this little operation was proceeding, I became more and more pleased with my new acquaintance. Never in my intercourse with young men of genius, had I met with an instance in which there was such entire absence of all pretension. In him the qualities of a highly-cultivated taste were united with most unassuming manners. Every subsequent visit confirmed the impression, and I resolved to hold fast by an acquaintance, that soon ripened into a friendship which continued without change or abatement to the last hour of life.

When the sketches for which I had asked his assistance were completed, I inquired what were his prospects, and whether his time was fully occupied. He replied, with great frankness, that he had nothing in prospect – nothing that would pay; the Illustrations of Essex,[4] on which he had been employed, had drawn to a close, and that he was anxious for a new engagement. I then proposed that if he would call upon me in the course of a few days, I might be able to suggest something worth his consideration. When he called again, I told him that my endeavours to serve him had signally failed; but I had been thinking much of Switzerland as a new field for his pencil. He immediately caught at the word, and as the ground was unoccupied, and the popular taste for illustrated works on the increase, we could not suppose but that the more striking scenes of Helvetian landscape, if well painted and described, would be no unwelcome boon to the British public. I had reason to believe that we could obtain the patronage of the Royal Family, as well as that of many others of rank and influence in the country; and the more we talked of the plan the more feasible it appeared. The first difficulty was to find a publisher, a man of taste and enterprise; but this being soon overcome, a prospectus was drawn up, and the first announcement of *Switzerland Illustrated*, was received in a manner that fully justified the undertaking.*

Thus encouraged, and impatient to reach the scene of his operations, Mr Bartlett started for Paris on the 12th of November [1832]. The season was unfavourable; but the object of his journey was so pressing, and the speculation so very

---

* In Germany, as well as France, it found immediate friends; and in Paris, the efforts of the late M. Marc-Antoine Jullien to give it popularity were completely successful. Nor ought I to forget the co-operation of a meritorious individual, Mr Christophe Mercier, who had faithfully served me in my various travels abroad. And when the first part was issued, its reception in the French metropolis was all that the artist and his publisher could desire.

promising, that he resolved to take possession of the ground at once, and passing rapidly through France he crossed the Jura and took up his residence at Geneva. On this journey he had the happiness to be accompanied by his wife, on whom the anxious and heavy task of watching at the bedside of her sick husband too suddenly devolved. His passage across the Swiss frontier in December, and his first impressions of the scenery are thus graphically described in his journal:

'As we slowly dragged up the steep ascent, the wind rattled the windows of the coach, and the deep roar of mountain torrents broke the stillness of midnight. The coach stopped at the door of an *auberge*, slippery with frost and snow; and, beyond the ruddy gleams of a huge fire of pine-logs, all seemed to recede into mysterious darkness. On a bench, by the crackling logs, we drank some hot wine and water, which sent a glow through our frames, cramped and chilled by sitting so long in the coach. In a few minutes the sledges were ready, and in one of these we were placed side by side. The postilion mounted, and, with a loud tinkling of bells, we dashed off through the snow drifts into the wide, mysterious waste. The night wind roared and swept up the drifted surface in fitful gusts, which whirled round the traineau; but yet we could not draw the curtains, such a charm was there in the novelty of our situation; the wild aspect of the mountain wilderness, dimly seen and interpreted by the imagination, the poles, placed along the road-side, half buried in snow, and but faintly discerned as they stretched away, were the only indicators of the road. The traineau presently sank into a deep and narrow track, just wide enough for one to pass at a time, and here we found ourselves in the forests of Jura.

'As we proceeded, the tall pines rose up on either hand; their dark, projecting boughs hung over our heads covered heavily with snow, which dropped in patches, as the slight motion of the traineau disturbed the perfect stillness; or settled in a shower of drops, as some slight gust of wind, penetrating the recesses of the forest, agitated the drooping branches. Dim as was the light, the maniform beauty of the snow-covered and crusted foliage did not escape us. Solemn, yet indescribably beautiful was the stillness: the soft sound of the traineau cutting its way through the snow, the tinkling of the bells, now lively, now reduced almost to silence – as at a slow pace we tracked some difficult pass through the cumbering heaps – seemed to deepen it. We could hear afar the moaning of the wind over the higher pine-clad region, seen duskily through the mists of night; but it did not reach us in our deep and sheltered recess.

'In the morning we entered upon the more open glades of the forest. All was dim around, but a vast and radiant glow was kindling behind the eastern peaks. The sunbeams soon glanced down from among the pines, and touched with ruddy glow the projecting roofs of a humble village, just awakening into life. The cock crowed cheerily, the smoke curled up from the chimneys, and a few peasants were seen at their early labour, carrying in piles of pine-tree logs. The icicles hung glittering from the roofs nearly to the ground. The horn sounded, and the traineau dashed up to the door of the *auberge*. The kitchen-fire of huge crackling logs received a fresh heap as we entered, and the hostess presented us with welcome beakers of hot milk.

'The sun was now abroad, bright and radiant upon the snow; the drops fell like showers of diamonds from the trees and roofs, glittering in the deep blue sky. Our new postilion looked gallant in red and blue; his horn sounded shrilly and lustily; and the horses rattling their bells, galloped out into the open snow. The sledge rolled from side to side, as it encountered the drifts, while merriment and laughter resounded behind, and had it even rolled over, our mirth would only have increased.

'Again, all day through the forests, by half-buried hamlets of pinewood, through mountain pasturages, whose fresh green sward here and there peeped timidly through its mantle of snow – and [through] deep valleys, black with endless pines, and studded with solitary châlots [chalets]. The air was keen and bracing. How is the tone of mind raised, when the harshness and littlenesses of common life are forgotten in communion with the solitary magnificence of nature, which infuses a thoughtful serenity – the true element for the unfolding of the higher nature – the preparation for her most profound teachings!

'Is there no end to these dusky forests, and their eternal clothing of pine? The evening clouds float in their golden hues behind the mountain summits; but no outlet yet appears to the world beyond. It was while nearing the summit of a long ascent, that we asked ourselves this question. The earth seemed cleft open from our very feet, when suddenly a dazzling vision burst upon us so vast – so confused – so shadowy – so indescribably glorious – that we could only look at each other in silent amazement.

'How describe in detail what the eye now took in at one glance – what the soul drank in, in one blissful moment? How find words to convey an idea of those wondrous Alps, soaring above plain and lake, and successive mountain ranges, into the serenity of a loftier heaven? Three thousand feet below us lay the deep basin of the azure Leman; with towns and spires, and the cheerful beauty of cultivated fields! A rich glow of dying light lay upon the lower mountains; but upon the region of eternal snows, lay rose-hues, beautiful as the last smile on the face of a departing saint, reflecting the gleams of an opening eternity.'

The point from which our young traveller caught the first view of the everlasting hills was near La Vattay; the scenery of which, as we descend to the gates of Geneva, has been fully described in the *Switzerland Illustrated*. We turn, therefore, to his arrival in the city of Calvin, where the enthusiasm with which he began and continued his sketches, at a most inclement season, brought on a long and dangerous illness, of which he has left the following notes:

'As our means were narrow, and strict economy was needful, after much research, we lighted upon an apartment in the fourth stage of a large, gloomy old house, which, however, rose directly out of the smiling waters of the lake. Our only assistant was an old woman, in an adjoining cabinet, whose infirmities had increased her natural harshness. Here, notwithstanding, we were very happy, ever anticipating the coming pleasures of our further progress through the glorious regions we already loved.

'This prospect was interrupted by an attack of fever, brought on by a cold, caught in the snow of the mountains, which, in a few days, became serious. It was a sad visitation for my wife; without friends, or even acquaintance, in the place; speaking French but indifferently, and having not only to seek out assistance, but do everything herself, for the crabbedness of our landlady seemed to increase with the progress of my malady. Accident directed us to Dr G–, for whose sympathising kindness, as well as professional skill, I shall ever feel grateful. Memory still presents me with snatches of delirium, and intervals in which I see the anxious face of my wife, and hear the cordial and cheerful voice of the physician, who had the art, in him I may call it nature, of relieving the mind by the exhibition of that sympathy which comes from the heart. He strove to raise the often fainting spirits of my wife, and alleviate her bitter anxiety – to the expression of which, besides himself, there was none to listen. It was well that she had lighted upon some one who could feel for her; for there was much for her to bear ... Not unfrequently was she obliged to go forth at night into the gloomy streets, with a lantern, to seek the physician through frost and snow – alarmed by the sudden relapses of the fever.

'At last I became convalescent, and was ordered to take gentle exercise. The winter was passing away; for though the snow still lay upon the mountains, the plains were free. Vernal airs began to temper the harshness of the season –

though cold gusts would still descend from the ravines, and lash up the waves of the lake into foam. My daily walk was to a rising ground beyond the walls commanding the outstretched lake and the long ranges of its sheltering mountains. Seated on a grassy bank, by the gentle waves, which chased each other to the shore, and sunned by the beam which whitened the broad sails, flitting like birds about the blue waters, I received with luxury the returning sensations of health, and existence. Hope weaved afresh vague and delicious visions which filled the imagination. As the sound of the far-off bells of the village churches, scattered about those unequalled shores, came up exquisitely softened on the ear, the mind wandered beyond the boundaries of the distant mountains, or the icy peaks, among the endless varieties of untired and wonderful nature.'

In a cheerful mood, the minor evils which beset a patient in his progress towards convalescence are thus humorously described:

'Among the bad effects of illness must be reckoned its producing a grievous disinclination to work on the part of the convalescent, though his recovery be even rapid, more particularly when the nature of his illness, as in my own case, may have confined him to his bed, and eke, to water-gruel, or similar compositions. How delicious, then, to his natural appetite, is the first *morceau* of delicate cookery! such as a stewed mutton chop and a light pudding! How he anticipates, in his dreams, the coming breakfast! how he watches the tardy clock for the appointed hour of dinner! and how does he enjoy that meal, which Frenchmen scoff at, his tea-and-toast! By degrees his debilitated intellects become adequate to the perusal of a book, or the composition of a letter. How delightfully do these fill up the intervals between meal-times! At length comes the injunction – "You must wrap up well, and go out to-morrow!" – an injunction, which, at first, seems impossible to act upon. But, difficulties got over, suppose a brilliant morning, and the patient on his walk. How lovely, how novel, everything appears! He seems to have regained the lively impressions of his earliest youth, to say nothing of the sevenfold increase of his appetite.'

In the course of a few weeks his active pencil had been employed on the finest scenery in the Swiss Cantons. His sketches were finished on the spot, sent home to the publisher, and placed in the hands of the engraver; so that the several processes of sketching, engraving, and printing were all going forward at the same moment.

As soon as the first drawings were received, a consultation was held at my house as to their merit, and the reception they were likely to meet with from the public. Among the company were several men whose approbation was no slight encouragement to the publisher in so large and expensive an enterprise. All were unanimous in predicting a successful issue, and no one spoke with more confidence than the late Comte D'Orsay,[5] so well known by his taste in the Fine Arts; and his opinion had no little weight in his own extensive circle. The consultation ended much to the encouragement of the proprietor, and March 1 [1833], was named as the day on which the work was to be laid before the public.

Having promised, when I first suggested the work to Mr Bartlett, that I would gladly afford himself and the publisher all the assistance in my power to set it fairly afloat, I undertook to write the descriptive text. The poet, Campbell, then a daily visitor in my family, was captivated by a work which brought forcibly to his mind the 'Land of Tell'; and, to express his good wishes, he volunteered the stanza which still serves as a motto to the various editions of the work, English and foreign, and continued to the last, one of Mr Bartlett's warmest admirers.

In less than four months from the time of his crossing the Jura, the first specimens of Mr Bartlett's *Switzerland* were before the public; but, from the work being supplied to subscribers only, it was considered by influential houses in the trade as a monopoly, and, consequently, deprived of their countenance and support. The publisher, however, had no cause to regret this step; for, in a note to Mr Bartlett, he writes, 'I have great pleasure in informing you, that Part 1 of *Switzerland*, was published on March 1, and is a decided hit. Through the kind exertions of Dr B[eattie], the Queen's name was obtained; and within ten days were added a thousand of the nobility and most influential names in the kingdom. Your name as an artist is established. The returns from the work will now meet the expenses. Of the kind, gentlemanly, and strenuous exertions of Dr B[eattie] for the success of the undertaking, I cannot speak in too high praise.'*

So much for the commencement of a work, with which, both at home and

* The work was immediately translated into French by M. De Bauclas; and into German, by John von Horn, DD, formerly Professor of Divinity in the University of Göttingen, and now of Hanover; both these gentlemen were then residing in London. The translations were made under my immediate care – printed, and widely circulated all over the Continent. I have now a specimen of a St Petersburg edition; but from that, as from all copies circulated in the Austrian dominions, the Censors had excluded everything regarding the battles of Freedom and the founders of Helvetian liberty.

abroad, the name of Bartlett is most creditably identified. He did not remain in England, however, long enough to enjoy the personal congratulations of his friends. Before Part x of the work appeared, he had accomplished a considerable portion of his first visit to the Holy Land, for which he had set out on January 2 [1834]. The journey was undertaken on commission from a City firm [H. Fisher, Son], well known for its illustrated works, and on tolerably fair terms. In pursuance of this engagement, accompanied by his wife, Mr Bartlett proceeded direct to Paris; thence, by the nearest route, to Naples, where they had letters of introduction, and spent a short time on those delicious shores. He then took leave of Mrs Bartlett, who returned reluctantly to England – a very unpleasant, if not perilous journey for a lady – for, at the time she reached Lyons, the revolution was at its height, and she was placed in situations of no ordinary alarm. From Naples Mr Bartlett engaged a passage to Malta, and thence, after some delay, to Alexandria, where he landed in safety, and found letters from home announcing the great popularity of his *Switzerland*. Thus encouraged, he looked forward to other works which might secure not only fame but independence, and began his Syrian excursions in that happy union of health and spirits to which he was too frequently a stranger. The result of his journey is already before the public;[6] but from his private letters we select a few paragraphs which may be interesting to the reader.

'*Beyrout, June* 15, 1834 – After three weeks' detention at Alexandria, I set sail, in company with three English and one American gentleman, for Syria. We hired a vessel to ourselves and took our own provisions on board – living, in fact, very comfortably. After five days had elapsed, we got near the coast. I was sleeping on the deck on my carpet, and awaking at dawn, descried the long mountain outline of the coast of Palestine. As we neared it, the flat shore advanced, and the hills receded; it was not particularly striking. Our stupid captain, however, instead of making Jaffa, ran by mistake nearly fifty miles to the south, along the coast of the Philistines, which is quite desolate. Gaza appeared on a hill-top, and we ran past the ruins of the far-famed Askelon. The sea-coast is flat and sandy; at length Jaffa appeared, built on a hill projecting into the sea – a melancholy-looking town, but with more verdure in the environs than usual. After some delay we landed, and went to the house of the English consul, who received us most hospitably. Here fresh disasters awaited us, for we learned that the whole mountain country of Palestine was in a formidable state of insurrection, and that to go to Jerusalem was impossible. Ibrahim Pasha himself, with his troops, was encamped without the town, waiting the arrival of fresh regiments, in order to put down the insurgents. We went to pay our respects, and learnt the truth of the case. Passing through the narrow, dirty bazaars of the town, and gaining the outside of the wall, I was quite satisfied at the glowing luxuriance of Eastern foliage which presented itself. The palm, pomegranate, fig, vine, cypress, and other trees of whose names I was ignorant, composed a splendid mass of verdure. In a short time we gained the Pasha's camp, and a most lively scene it proved. His own tent was pitched on an eminence by the sea, close to an old mosque, which he had also furnished. Around were the tents of his officers and soldiers; some embedded in foliage, some on the brow of the hill: arms piled, horses grazing, soldiers regaling themselves, while the officers were reposing, and smoking in the shade of the trees. We were ushered, without ceremony, into his tent, and then had full time to scrutinise the famous chief, who carried his triumphant arms well nigh to the walls of Stamboul. He looked much like a jolly butcher; but yet there was a something more: something of command – much of cunning – more of sensuality. He was very polite, and his friend, Omar Effendi, who was educated at Cambridge, informed us that we might, if we liked, accompany him to Jerusalem, as he was only waiting for the ships, to which he pointed, as one by one they crowded sail and entered the roads. We then left him, and, in the evening, had much deliberation as to our plans. At length, we decided upon going up to Acre by water, and visiting that part of the coast before Jerusalem.' Accordingly, he proceeds to narrate, they left Jaffa at midnight in an Arab boat, and coasted along as far as Acre, whence the whole party made an excursion to Mount Carmel.

'On our return,' he continues, 'we were told that the Arabs, to the number of several thousands, had besieged the town, and that the road was dangerous. In spite of this, Mr Hammersley, the American gentleman, and myself, determined to proceed, and arrived safely in the evening in a village near Tyre, and slept under a shed. We next got on through Tyre, and slept near Sidon, in a hut; then passed through Sidon, and went up into the mountain to see Lady Stanhope. As the sun set we approached Djouni, and Mr Hammersley sent on his card; for myself, knowing that Lady Stanhope does not receive English, I went to a neighbouring village, and slept under a tree. Next morning, I met Hammersley, who had found a gracious reception; and after a ride in the mountains returned with him to Djouni, and was introduced to Lady Stanhope, who showed us the gardens; and again, after dinner, we conversed for some hours. She is a strange old lady – her head quite turned with astrology. She said I had a good star, and should rise about the middle of my life; that I was of a cheerful disposition, always disposed to see things favourably; very passionate now and then; and that I had better take care, or she would let out more. Strange things are to occur shortly; the Messiah is to come, and the bad man too, whom, it seems, she knows; with a great deal more of it. She entertained us very hospitably, and the next morning we left, and reached Beyrout in the evening. Travelling here is the strangest mixture of fun, danger, inconvenience, good living, and starving. One night we are entertained in a convent, and live in clover; the next finds us in a village khan, sleeping under a shed, and supping on milk and eggs; a third, we are dining and supping out. Sometimes kept all night awake by fleas – the next sleeping like a top in good sheets. We jog on about twenty miles a day on horseback, walking chiefly, for I cannot yet trot well. At Beyrout we have met with many friends. The American missionaries have entertained us hospitably.'

On leaving Beyrout, Mr Bartlett followed the sea-shore to Tripoli, then ascended the steeps of Lebanon; slept in the house of the Sheik of Eden; examined the Cedars, and descended into the plain of Coelo-Syria, at the further extremity of which appeared the temples of Baalbec. Here he slept in a cavern: next morning he felt unwell, but went on and spent the whole day examining the temples. At sunset he went to Mr Catherwood's encampment at the head of a stream, and there passed the night. Next morning he was seized with ague, and a tendency to brain fever. He was then removed to a ruinous upper chamber in a Saracenic castle, adjoining the great temple. His servant being afraid to remain alone with him during the night, Mr Bonomi, who was with Mr Catherwood,[7] agreed to come every night and watch with him.* Next day an English physician, Dr Whitely, fortunately arrived, who shaved his head and prescribed for him. In a few days, though the attack was severe, he was able to creep about a little, and to make some sketches.

His intended visit to Jerusalem – the chief object of this journey – was entirely defeated by the open war, in which the Holy City had been taken and

---

* 'When the bats, rising from the vaults below, began to flit through the chamber, I used to hear the cheering cry of my friend Bonomi echoing through the winding passage ... And never did a sick child thrill more at his mother's voice than I at the hearty, "Well, how are you, old fellow?" which issued from his lips as he burst into the dreary apartment. Then the lamps were lighted, the pistols primed, Antonio planted on his mattress across the entrance, and everything made snug for the night.' [*Footsteps*, p. 45] sacked by the insurgents. From Baalbec, therefore, he proceeded to Antioch and to Tarsus. In his passage, by an open boat, of fifteen days along the coast of Asia Minor, to Adalia, he was again seized with a dangerous fever, from which he narrowly escaped. The stirring incidents of this perilous journey are all detailed with graphic effect in his subsequent works – *Syria*, and the *Footsteps*.

Having completed his tour in Syria, and taken sketches of all the biblical and classical scenes in his route, both outward and homeward, Mr Bartlett, after an absence of twelve months, returned to London in January [1835]. He had performed his engagements greatly to the satisfaction and subsequent emolument of his publisher, and immediately began to prepare his sketches for the engraver. By the time these were completed, a new field was opening for the exercise of his talents – a history of the Waldenses, illustrated in the same manner as Switzerland.

Early in April, therefore, he proceeded to the Valleys, where he was most kindly received and encouraged by the pastors, whose character, wants, and patient endurance of many wrongs, had become known to the British public, through the able pen of Dr Gilly.[8] Once in the Valleys, Mr Bartlett visited every scene connected with the history and persecutions of that remarkable people, who, flattered by the object of his visit, did everything to facilitate his labours. Of the success which attended him in this enterprise, the book itself is a monument. In the autumn of the same year I attended the tri-centenary Jubilee of the Reformation at Geneva, and crossing the Great St Bernard, made a tour in the Protestant Valleys, to collect materials for the work. I had thus most satisfactory evidence of the lifelike fidelity with which Mr Bartlett had transferred to paper the striking scenes* of Waldensian history.

During his brief sojourn among the pastors of these romantic valleys, he made every man his friend; and when he took leave, he was followed by the prayers of the whole Protestant community. Among the high Alps, his first meeting with M. Ehrmann is thus recorded: 'Having slept at Guillestre, I next morning ascended the pass of the Guil, one of the most terrible in the Alps, and richly deserving of my attention in point of scenery. I then entered the valley of Arvieu;[9] and, on passing the church, I observed a person before me, dressed in black, of whom I asked for the dwelling of M. Ehrmann, the successor of Felix Neff. It

---

* Among the illustrations of this work, are a considerable portion by my late friend Mr Brockedon, FRS, well known to every classic reader by his *Passes of the Alps*.

was the worthy pastor himself; and being near his house, he invited me in. It is a very humble abode, though certainly the best in La Chalp. We ascended to a small chamber, which, in its furniture and arrangement, wore an air of decent poverty. The book shelves, however, were well furnished. No person was in the room on our arrival; so the pastor immediately put his hand to the good work of preparing dinner. His wife and his mother then came in, and we all sat down to a frugal but cheerful meal. I soon found that I was in a house where everything had a strict reference to religion; and my new friend was most kind, gentle, and cheerful. He then proposed to me to accompany him to a public meeting at Brunichard, a hamlet at a short distance, but higher up the valley.

'Starting immediately, we soon arrived at a collection of wild pine huts, of a squalid and dingy appearance. On entering one of these by a low aperture, serving as a door, we sank into a soft carpeting of straw and litter, and stumbled forward into a dim, dark hovel, the temperature of which was close almost to suffocation. At first I could distinguish nothing; but at length I made out a long stable filled with horses, cows, sheep, and goats. At the further end, seated under the struggling light of a small window, was the family group – their pallid faces turned eagerly towards the door. Upon the pastor's proposing a *re-union*, I saw that all were not equally disposed to attend to it. Some, however, ran to apprise the neighbouring cottagers. We then repaired to another and rather lighter dwelling; and the pastor, with two or three of the elders, placing themselves near the light, the rest, as they entered, ranged along quite into the middle of the hovel. It was a scene for Rembrandt himself! the dim struggling light upon the worn but strongly-marked countenances of those dwellers in the Alpine wild, the deep obscurity of the background, the cattle and agricultural implements faintly seen – all presented a combination never to be forgotten.

'A portion of scripture was then selected and read by one of the young men present. The pastor then gave out a hymn, and himself setting the tune, the blended voices of old and young arose from the midst of a stable to the worship of the true God. The prayer and the sermon were indeed excellent – simple, fervent, and practical – admirably adapted to the place and people.

'The service being concluded, mutual greetings passed between the pastor and his mountaineers as well as their visitor. I soon observed that with a wisdom always in season, the pastor "mingled God in all his discourse"; and many were his words of advice or consolation, for to him they applied in all their domestic troubles.

'As we walked home, I observed to M. Ehrmann, that it seemed deplorable that the peasantry should live in so dirty and wretched a condition; and that it would be highly desirable to give them better ideas of comfort and decency. But long habit, he replied, and jealousy of change, had thrown great difficulties in the way of ameliorating their condition, to which their great poverty also contributed. Indeed, these poor mountaineers have little beyond the means of a bare existence. In proportion, however, as their minds have been elevated by the influence of the Gospel, they have become more persuadable on this point.

'The evening passed away cheerfully at the pastor's fireside. We had two or three visitors from the village, one of whom, a young woman, seemed actuated by a most fervent piety, though apparently diffident and reserved in the presence of "the stranger." I was surprised at some of her observations, and the prayer she offered up in the evening, by desire of the pastor, was extraordinary for its warmth and force of expression. Remarkable as are the gifts of some of these villagers, caution is doubtless necessary in their exercise. This was admitted by M. Ehrmann; and I remember having seen fragments of letters from Neff to his flock at Dormeilleuse, enjoining prudence. Here Christianity appears to have had a wonderful effect in promoting intellectual growth, as well as temporal comfort, among these poor but worthy mountaineers.

'The chamber in which I slept was that occupied by Neff,* very small, and the plaster still rough. The rain detained me indoors all Friday, but early on Saturday morning the pastor prepared to go up to San'-Veran, for the service of the ensuing Sabbath. A blouse, or frock of gray stuff, covered his well-worn garments; over his shoulder he slung a capacious bag, with some articles of apparel and a number of tracts and New Testaments, and kissing his wife and mother, he led the way.

'Taking leave of the presbytery of Neff, where I had received the most kind and hearty welcome, I followed my worthy host. The clouds were still low on the mountains, but the air was deliciously fresh in those high regions. I was now well acquainted with my companion, a man admirably adapted for his laborious charge. I could not have spent an hour in his company, without discovering that his whole delight – like that of his predecessor – was in the unwearied labours of his office.'

* Felix Neff, pastor of the High Alps. For a most interesting memoir of this Christian hero, we are indebted to the Rev. Dr Gilly. It has the interest of a romance, with the gravity of an apostolic epistle.

Having completed the series of Waldensian sketches, Mr Bartlett returned to London; but, in his way home, taking advantage of a new route, he added to his portfolio much Alpine scenery which did not come within the scope of his new work. In all his previous and subsequent travels – Jerusalem alone excepted – nothing pleased him more than this visit to the Protestant Valleys of Piedmont.

A new illustrated work on the Netherlands having been projected, Mr Bartlett went over to Brussels in November [1835], and there commenced the series of views which subseqeuntly appeared in the *History and Scenery of the Low Countries*, by Professor van Kampen.

After returning from the Low Countries, Mr Bartlett remained at home only a month. His name, as an artist, was exceedingly popular. Everything to which he lent the charm of his pencil, was crowned with success; and, thus encouraged, the publisher resolved upon another extensive work, to be called the *Scenery of America*. The idea was suggested by Mr N.P. Willis, to whom I had the pleasure of introducing Mr Bartlett; and between the poet and the artist, a friendship soon sprang up which greatly promoted the success of the new enterprise.

In April [1836], Mr Bartlett went to Paris, where his *Switzerland*, and other works, were in extensive circulation. The former, translated from my text by M. de Bauclas, met with a most flattering reception; while *Scotland Illustrated*, the companion work, promised a success little inferior to that of *Switzerland*. Both works were patronized in the highest circles, and noticed with great favour by the French press. The principal agent of the publisher was the late M. Ferrier – an officer who had served with great credit and distinction under Napoleon. He had been wounded at Waterloo, and, on quitting the army, endeavoured to improve his domestic circumstances, by engaging in literary commissions, of which that in question turned out much to his advantage.

During his brief sojourn in Paris, Mr Bartlett was introduced to M. de Lamartine; but he found the poet so surrounded by members of the Chamber, that he had very little conversation with him. He was much gratified, however, by having made the acquaintance of a man whose *Pilgrimage in the Holy Land*,[10] he had perused among the very scenes which inspired it.

From New York, he writes: 'You would have been delighted with part of the passage in the beautiful ship I went out in from Havre, with more than 30 cabin passengers, 220 steerage, besides crew. We had some heavy gales, but it was magnificent to see the workings of the mighty ocean. I remember one evening when the sea ran tremendously high – vessel under reefed topsails, every wave seemed impending over us, ready to sink us into the abyss. It looked awful at first, but to see the gallant ship riding unhurt upon the foamy crests of the tremendous waves, to hear the wind whistle shrilly through the cordage, all in faultless order – fear gave way to admiration and excitement. Then, sometimes in the evening, when the vessel was moving on majestically with her tall spires of canvas rocking in the twilight sky, I got on the ship's side and marked her beautiful motion through the waves, the swelling of the sails in the evening breeze, our lady passengers out on deck with their skipping ropes, the stars coming forth – it was gloriously fine! And then the approach to land, the spicy smell of the air, at last the fresh grassy odour from the distant shore, the light breezes throwing up the playful waves against the ship's side to dissolve into showers of silvery spray! Oh, the ocean is full of wonders, and you would delight to witness them.'

'*October* 23rd [1836] – It would be nonsense to try to describe Niagara, but I suppose you expect it. Chauteaubriand says it is rather a sea than a river; and he is right. You are in the thick woods, but you hear a mighty noise – the voice of many waters; your heart beats, you break through the trees. My God! what work is this? Hast Thou just let loose old ocean from his dark prison, that his waves thus career with madness of joy and glorious power? No, it is a river before me – a stupendous river, tossing its mighty waves, and hurrying on with a force that is irresistible to all but the voice of God! And *you* rush on, scarce knowing what you do: you follow this terrible river, while the spray from the mad waves falls on your brow like the playful stroke of a giant. On you rush with the wave; it disappears and you are on the edge of the precipice! The wind, the spray, beats in your face; the spray rising in vast clouds from the tremendous abyss, and soaring up to the serene sky like "everlasting incense!" I cannot describe the scene, but I can tell you that you would be so transported, as to wish to be an unbodied spirit, to mix with the wild delight of the waters, to ride on the cease-lessly-mounting spray, and toss on the dim white waves far below, twisted together like foes in a death-grapple but never ending their strife. Such is the fascination of this glorious, this unequalled spectacle! And when you seek at length soberly to measure the sight, it grows upon you; the roar seems to increase, the water to dilate, the solid earth to tremble. But it is folly to attempt to give you an idea; one thing is certain, I longed for you to be there, and to see you enjoy it! It is, indeed, to see God in the excellency of His power. There are moments when you seem to doubt the reality of what you view; and, in short,

119

you may dream of Niagara, but words will never describe it to you. "I have seen Niagara," says Miss F. Kemble, "and it is useless to say more."'

In this excursion Mr Bartlett spent a short time with Mr N.P. Willis, at his charming villa on the Susquehanna; and in his society made a pilgrimage to the classic scenes of *Wyoming*.[11] To this visit the poet has made gratifying illusion in his *Letters from under a Bridge*; and so pleased was our traveller with the manner of living in that region, that for a time he entertained serious thoughts of taking out his family, and settling in the States. The intention, however, was overruled; and after an absence of twelve months, Mr Bartlett recrossed the Atlantic in July [1837]. But it was to spend only a few anxious days in the bosom of his family; for, during his absence in the United States, a new work, the *Beauties of the Bosphorus*, having been projected, he made preparations for a second journey to the East. The serious illness and privations, to which he had been subjected in his former visit, were not forgotten; but as nothing more eligible was to be had at the time, he had no alternative but to accept the enter-prize with all its attendant risks. On the present occasion, however, he was to have the companionship of a very old and warm friend, the late Mr Thomas Lemon, of Messrs Coutts's,[12] whose delicate health was expected to profit by change of climate. This arrangement was the best that could be desired. About the middle of August they met in Paris, and, after a few days spent among the galleries of the Louvre, the churches, and other objects of paramount interest, they started for the East.

From a late friend, many years ambassador in Constantinople, I had the pleasure of procuring, in favour of Mr Bartlett, letters of introduction to the Turkish minister, from whom he obtained facilities rarely conceded to any British artist. From the Countess of B–[13] he had also a letter of introduction to Namich Paçha; and, furnished with these, and other means of personal inter-course with the Turkish authorities, our talented artist had every encouragement to prosecute his researches. The following are extracts from his private letters, dated Smyrna and Constantinople.

'*Smyrna* – Call that Greek boatman, jump into his gondola, pass under the guns of that English frigate, and admire "the flag that braved a thousand years, the battle and the breeze," flaunting nobly in the peerless blue of the Orient. Thread your way through the first snug vessels from Britain or America, and by this time you will be *vis-à-vis* the Turkish quarter with its peculiar houses, mosques, and minarets, and will soon arrive at the extremity of the town. Passing a vast barrack, you land on a broken shore, at the foot of the Jewish burial ground. I will defy the most mercurial observer not to feel a sadness invading his senses, as he looks up to this mass of ruinous tombs – distinguishable from the white arid rock in which they are inserted – and then to the deep, dark, moveless cones of cypress, rising in solemn amphitheatre and looking down on an old quarter of half-ruinous houses, scarcely better than tombs. It strikes upon the most joyous spirits a gloom like that of the funereal trees themselves standing stark and changeless under a sky of the most resplendent light, and insensible to the soft and balmy air of the climate. As you slowly ascend among these mouldering tombs to the summit of an arid hill, no one, who has not seen these contrasts of the East, can imagine the effect of the dark groves with the tombs lying under their shadows.

'The view from this point is fine. Smyrna lies below; but its huddling together of flat roofs, broken only here and there by a tall, white minaret, looks little like the commercial "queen of Asia." An old castle, crowning the heights, has a grand effect; but the blue sea – the finely-formed but uncertain mountains opposite – with Mytelene and Seid in the distance, contribute the chief attractions. You may see flitting to and fro among the tombs, the women enveloped in long white robes, their faces covered with black veils, looking all like mourners. Yonder a few straggling peasants are lazily ascending the rocky hill, and the sound of their heavy hoofs, the buzzing of the wild bee, and the monotonous hum of the *cicala* among the cypresses, are the only sounds heard on this lonely height.

'By passing, however, between the enclosures of tombs you come upon the caravan route, and there the scene is often lively; trains of camels are seen proceeding with measured step – the tinkling of their bells, meanwhile, producing a singularly wild effect. The sunsets at Smyrna, in September and October, are peculiarly gorgeous. You see the light flashing between the solemn masses of cypress, or tinging the pale olive with a golden glow; while the thousand tombs, for the most part ruinous, are fringed with wild flowers.

'The Marina has the unequivocal recommendation of being the most airy spot in Smyrna. When the Mediterranean is agitated by a gentle breeze, the light caiques of the Greeks, with their gondola-looking boats, are seen flitting about, their sails catching the soft but brilliant light of Asia – with the vessels in the bay, and beyond, the beautifully formed mountains. Here are groups of Armenians in grave robes, Kalpacks sleek and respectable, Greek boatmen, stray Turks, Franks in white jackets and straw hats, semi-Frank natives – not forgetting parties of English officers in white, buff, and blue – all tight and compact. When all this is to be seen from my window, he who looks out of it will forget that the floor is uncarpeted, the furniture cracked and tawdry, and the whole arrangement very desultory and uncomfortable.

'In general, the Frank quarter of an oriental town is the least interesting, void of character and expression. The natives engaged in European commerce adulterate their style by the introduction of various articles of dress, and forms of speech, which spoil them wholly; and the Franks themselves get so mystified, that it is often difficult to decide whether they are Franks or natives. The Marina is very well to fall back upon for whatever semblance is to be had of English comfort and social intercourse; but it is in the bazaars, the cemeteries, or in the lonely wastes around them, where the camel-bell is heard, or the caravan is seen winding into the city, that the traveller must look for the wild and stirring excitements of Oriental life, for all that he is to remember hereafter.

'A peculiarly solitary and beautiful spot is that near the cemetery and gateway, with the adjoining fountain, the luxuriant freshness of the gardens, and the tombs constantly visited by mourners and adorned with flowers. I visited the Stadium with Armenian missionaries, and saw a spot of reputed sanctity – an altar on which it is customary, when any one dies, to place the body and make an oration over it. The Greek Church of St John is rich in carving: around are dark lanes, dry fountains, and ruins of a theatre – all peculiarly solitary. In ascending to the Stadium are seen the tombs of those who have perished during the plague. As you return from these scenes, you hear the cry of the muezzin from above; and in moving on, you are struck with the silence of deserted bazaars. The liveliest scene is at the Caravan Bridge. Here are smart cafés, constant troops of passengers: gaily attired Franks and Greeks, toil-worn, dark camel-drivers, sleek Armenians, blind beggars, Turkish women of the lower class with peculiar complexions, something like that of a peach in shadow. This is the gayest spot in Smyrna.'

'*Constantinople, October* 1 [1837] – The plague had just ceased when we got to Smyrna; and there is not much here. However, it is always like a sword suspended over one's head. We do not remain many days longer in this city, which, after all, I regret leaving. It is so beautiful that I sometimes think I am dreaming. Pera, where we lodge, is an indescribable quarter – everything is mongrel; the very dogs, which one tumbles over in the street, seem to have lost all pith, and can do nothing but bark – and they *do* bark in style, but never bite. We live in cemeteries, heaving with recently interred plague victims, and the remains of houseless dogs, dead from starvation or ill-treatment. The refuse of the place makes Pera a paradise for those who like strong excitement of the nasal organs. The lanes are breakneck, and in bad weather perilous to pass from slipperiness; yet when we get out of Pera, we have the finest views in the world, with the sea washing round Constantinople! – But why attempt to describe what Byron himself gave up?'

In March, the following year, after an absence of seven months, Mr Bartlett returned from the East. In his voyage home, he touched at the more celebrated islands of the Archipelago; and, on arriving in Sicily, a new and interesting field was thrown open for his pencil. The sketches taken on this occasion were originally intended to illustrate a classical history of Sicily; but the project was unhappily abandoned.

After a brief sojourn with his family, of only a few weeks, arrangements were entered into with his publisher for a second tour in the United States, but chiefly in Canada.

On this occasion, Mr Bartlett embarked at Liverpool, and after a tempestuous voyage, and much personal risk, arrived at his destination.

In a letter, dated *Bytown, Canada, August* 26 [1838], he writes: 'You have heard of my safe arrival at New York. I soon after started for Canada, and have got on pretty well with the exception of a day or two's illness, which, though rather serious, was taken in time. I now expect to be some two or three weeks before I go to Mr Willis's farm to spend a few days, and look a little about me. He wishes me to settle in his neighbourhood, and I am anxious to study the subject a little, in order to be able to form a fair estimate of the expenses and difficulties.'

From this period, until December, he was employed in making sketches on the spot for *Canadian Scenery*, and with what success was fully demonstrated by the subsequent popularity of that elegant work.

By the end of December [1838], Mr Bartlett was again at home – but not to enjoy the domestic repose for which he yearned. He was speedily urged to undertake a journey into Scotland, to supply the firm with views, for completing their *Scotland Illustrated*, a work on which, during Mr Bartlett's absence, they had engaged the talents of Mr Allom; and also for a new series of *Ports and Harbours*.[14] From this period until the first of June [1839], he was engaged in finishing his sketches of Canada, Scotland, and a portion of the Oriental Scenes.

In June, a work on Ireland,[15] similar to that on Switzerland, was projected; and having entered into new arrangements to furnish drawings for the undertaking, Mr Bartlett and Mr N.P. Willis, who had engaged to write the historical and descriptive text, repaired to Dublin at the same time.

After his return from Ireland, where he had made a personal inspection of all that is most remarkable in its scenery and antiquities, Mr Bartlett spent the winter at his own cheerful hearth – a happiness which he had too seldom enjoyed – and in May [1840], took his family to Ramsgate. There he passed the ensuing autumn and winter – much pleased with the sea and coast scenery – receiving his friends, and sedulously attending to the health and education of his children.

Here an intimate friend and I paid him a visit at his cottage, in the picturesque village of St Lawrence, and never shall I forget the pleasure we felt in his society and conversation during the two brief days we enjoyed it. His works were then translated and widely circulated abroad: at home they were to be seen on every table; while the criticisms of the press were all that could gratify honourable ambition, and stimulate his genius to still higher efforts.

Encouraged by the popularity which had attended his labours – popularity which never deserted him – he had good reason to expect that, by some future and more lucrative enterprize, he might at least be enabled to realize for his young family a moderate independence. This was his first and last ambition; but it was again and again defeated by circumstances over which he had no control.

A third visit to the United States having been proposed to him, Mr Bartlett again took leave of his family, and in the month of March [1841] embarked for New York. After another extensive tour in the Northern and Southern States – during which nothing was overlooked that could minister to the public taste in a department in which he so eminently excelled – he returned home at the close of the year. His destiny, however, was not to rest so long as health and activity enabled him to continue the many risks and privations of foreign travel. His taste and inclination, at this time, were to limit his excursions, to turn to the best account he might the experience and fruits of previous wanderings, and to seek in the bosom of his family that happiness which had hitherto been so cruelly interrupted. His heart and affections were centred at home; but the necessity of making provision for that home by often-repeated journeyings abroad, had almost reduced him to the life of an exile.

Having completed the drawings for *Canadian Scenery*, Mr Bartlett entered into fresh engagements for a new work; and, early in the following year [1842], proceeded to the Danube. Hence the *Danube Illustrated* the sketches for which, commencing with the Black Forest, terminated at the Black Sea, and comprised all the most striking scenery with which the banks of that majestic river abound.

But the grand object of this tour, which had been defeated by civil war in the previous journey, was to make a minute survey of Jerusalem – a task which he now accomplished with even more than his usual success. His heart was in the subject; and the *Walks* fully demonstrate how well his mind had been trained and prepared for the production of a work which is admirably adapted to the use of religious and biblical readers. This was the first work on which his *pen* as well as his pencil had been employed; and we could have no better evidence with what skill and ability he adapted the one to the other, so as to produce the most pleasing and efficient results. I had frequently urged him to make this experiment; but no persuasion could overcome his natural diffidence, until, driven to it by a fortunate accident, he draw up the first of that series of pen and pencil sketches so justly admired for its rare combination of literary and artistic excellence. During this tour in the East, Mr Bartlett took sketches of the Archipelago, Rhodes, Cyprus, Beyrout, Jaffa, and many others of biblical and classic celebrity.

On his return to Alexandria, July 22nd [1842], he writes: 'I have now visited Jerusalem and a large portion of the Holy Land, without danger or difficulty, and am now in the 'Land of Egypt' safe and sound. I landed at Beyrout, in Syria, which is the port of Damascus, in [sic] about two days' journey thence over Mount Lebanon. I then coasted to Jaffa, and in about eighteen hours arrived at Jerusalem, where I found a very kind old friend,* who was acting as consul, and also architect to the new church. He received me very kindly, and insisted on my boarding with him during my stay, which accordingly was very pleasant. We went together to Bethlehem and Hebron. I then joined a party† to see the Jordan and the Dead Sea. After another week in the Holy City, I set off alone to Nazareth and the Lake of Tiberias; and then, cutting down from Safed to Acre, returned by sea to Beyrout. My tour was not extensive, but I need not say most

---

* F.W. Johns, Esq.

† See Madame Pfeiffer's account. [Ida (Reyer) Pfeiffer, *Visit to the Holy Land, Egypt, and Italy*, tr. H.W. Dulcken ... London, Ingram, Cooke, 1852].

interesting. I found Jerusalem more striking than I had expected, as a sight; and the pleasure of visiting such places as Bethel, Sichem, Nazareth, Hebron, and many others – Bible in hand – was, perhaps, greater than any I ever enjoyed in travel. If I reach home safely, it will be delightful to recall and talk it over.

'Being so near Cairo and the Pyramids, I cannot resist the temptation of visiting these famous places. But I am at present in quarantine – most absurdly so – because, in fact, I have just come from Beyrout, where there is *no* plague, to Alexandria, where there is always *some* plague, and still am supposed to require purification.'

It was in this journey that Mr Bartlett made the acquaintance of the celebrated Madame Ida Pfeiffer, who, in her *Travels round the World*, lately published, makes frequent and honourable mention of the English traveller. Some interesting particulars of this amiable and enterprising lady were afterwards given by Mr Bartlett in *Sharpe's Magazine*.[16] From the conclusion of this journey until 1845, he was engaged in miscellaneous literary work.

In his posthumous narrative of this period, he writes: 'My publisher continued to employ me for some years on the same class of publications, all of which were more or less successful, and at a higher rate of remuneration; but one which, owing to the expense of travelling, never enabled me to obtain more than a mere livelihood upon a very economical footing. I did, indeed, contrive to lay by a few hundred pounds in the course of some ten years; but, just as I had done so, the trade, by which the publisher had, after working it successfully for years, already obtained a fortune, became slack; and he was unwilling to enter upon any fresh speculation. It now fell out, as is too often the case with precarious occupations like mine, that the branch I had taken up never gave me enough to lay by even the smallest independence; and I was unable successfully to enter upon any other branch of the profession. I had already been for my publisher on a journey to Palestine, with the view to the publication of a similar serial to the others; but owing to the badness of the times as he said, the work was laid by for the present. It was afterwards published under the title of *The Christian in Palestine*.

'It was under these circumstances I was sent abroad, at my own suggestion, to collect materials for the two works – *Forty Days in the Desert*, and the *Nile Boat*. The first of these publications decidedly raised my reputation as a writer, and several editions have been sold of it.' In the early part of this year Mr Bartlett made a second tour in Ireland, to select illustrations for Mr and Mrs Hall's popular work,[17] and then started for the East.

On his arrival at Cairo, August 8th, 1845, he writes: 'Since leaving Paris, I have been quite well, with the exception of a few days' indisposition here, in consequence of too careless an exposure to the burning sun, which, at this season, is not to be braved with impunity. I am now quite restored, and about to ascend the Nile to Thebes and the Cataracts. "My boat is on the shore," or, at least, under water, to drown the rats and other vermin that may have taken berths for a passage with me. Unhappily, there is no drowning the light-winged mosquitoes, which are the worst of all, my hands being kept in a continual state of irritation by their stings. The plagues of Egypt are still in existence; but the progress of civilization has done something for travellers. The Indian mail route has given rise to much comfort, with good hotels, even to donkey-boys that speak English: for instance, the little imp that conducts me about, only ten years old, was standing by me while sketching, when a water-vender passed by, of whom I took a draught, and told the boy to pay him five *paras*, 1/4 *piastre*. When a bystander saw this, he made some observation to the boy in Arabic, to which he warmly retorted. I asked him what it meant? and received this explanation: "He tell me the master say you give him *half* a piastre, and you give him five paras, teep the rest. I tell him, how you know? you be dam!" From this you will see the English language is making progress here.

'You have no idea what numbers of things are wanted to go up the Nile. It is like furnishing a house: everything down to a rat-trap, cat, and goat for milk. It is a real Robinson Crusoe's palace, a Nile boat. I am told that I may expect a capsize, and so keep a cushion and strap ready, in case of finding myself suddenly immersed. You've heard, by the way, that in going from Marseilles to Malta, our steamer ran down a brig, which sank in a quarter of an hour, just giving time to save the crew. Heaven preserve me from more such adventures!

'Sunday here is very dull. I shall dine alone, with a black servant to wait upon me. "Would that I had a balloon *guidable*," as poor old F– used to say in a fit of enthusiasm; for then I would bring to for a few hours against the top of St Paul's and drop in just at dinner time. In one respect I beat you: all the population of Cairo streams past my window, and a very lively and amusing sight it presents.' After his return from the Cataracts, he writes:

'*Cairo, September* 28th [1845] – I can assure you travelling here is now outrageously dear, and increasingly so, owing to the liberality of lords with long purses, and to the great increase in comforts. I could most joyfully have given you the other bench in my cabin, and made a chum of you in my six weeks' cruise up to the first Cataracts of the Nile. We might have made a better work of it together; for I confess I found it lonely at times. You have a boat about forty feet long, with cabins like this – [gives a sketch] – with one master-cabin, having two benches, on one of which you arrange your mattress – a bed by night, a sofa by day; and on the other lie your books, etc. Beyond this is a smaller sort of niche, where you dress; and beyond this again is a third place, where you stow away things. You have to bring everything, even pots and kettles, plates, dishes, and provisions, and also to carry a goat for milk. Thus provided, you travel very comfortably. My manner of life was this: awaking before sunrise, when it is always delicious on the river, I jump up and perform ablutions, call for break-fast, fresh milk, and make coffee; cold fowl and the bread-cake of the villages toasted and buttered. Then, if sailing slowly and wind a-head, I jump ashore in shirt and trousers, slippers, and no stockings, armed with a sort of pike, and walk a mile or two along the bank by the villages and palm-groves, which are very beautiful. I had a bunch of dates hung up in my cabin to nibble at. Then, if a temple turns up, I go and draw it – always having a large umbrella stuck in the ground – for you are here, my friend, almost under the tropic, and in the hot sun. You have dinner at twelve: excellent soup, Irish stew, roast fowls and potatoes; roast or boiled mutton; pigeons, salad and custards, or other small matter, a cup of coffee, and sometimes curry. Then tea at five, and to bed at dark. I was much struck with Thebes, and pleased with the scenery about the Cata-racts; but when I see you again, I shall be better able to enter into details.

'I am now about to start for Mount Sinai, perhaps for Petra; unless the great expense should deter me. I shall be obliged to take two servants, six camels, two tents, and provisions; more pots, water-skins, water-bottles, and things the existence of which I was not conscious of until I had to pay for them. So follow me in idea upon a jolting dromedary with water-bottle, to which I am constantly applying. Behold my evening-halt by some palm and fountain: the pitching of tents, and making tea with brushwood of the Desert! What adds great interest to this journey and Sinai is this: that a German professor, and others before him, fix on another mountain as the *real* Sinai, which rival crag I shall make it my business to examine particularly, Bible in hand. But enough of my own doings. In six or nine weeks I trust to see you again – exchanging this now delicious climate for the murky atmosphere of London. May we all meet again in peace!'

The result of this most interesting but perilous journey is fully embodied in the *Forty Days*, a work in which the united powers of artist and author are more strikingly developed than in any former or subsequent work on the subject.* It had the effect of immediately fixing his reputation; and, besides the high testimonies of the press, many complimentary letters reached him from private hands, which were filled with praise and encouragement. Amongst these was one from a lady, justly entitled the female Shakspeare of England [Joanna Baillie], which was peculiarly gratifying. I had sent for her perusal a copy of the *Desert*, and when returned to me, it was accompanied with a letter, from which an extract will be found in the Appendix.

On Mr Bartlett's return to London, his constitution was manifestly impaired by the effects of climate, to which he had nearly fallen a victim.† Every one was struck with the extraordinary change in his appearance. 'He seemed,' to use the words of his brother, 'twenty years older.' In his own personal narrative of the enterprise we have only indistinct allusions to any serious illness. His letters had not even named it; so that on his return home, it was only from its effects that we could form any opinion of its severity. But some time afterwards he wrote:

'In the last journey I irrecoverably damaged my constitution, and probably shortened my days. I came home, as everybody said only to die; and, indeed, my condition was pitiable.'

A little advice, however, which my knowledge of his constitution enabled me to offer, and his own confidence in the means employed were happily successful in gradually restoring him to tolerable health. He then applied with his usual alacrity to the arrangement of the valuable materials with which the recent journey had furnished him; and these were sufficient to employ both his pen and pencil.

For the benefit of his health, and the advantage of literary retirement, Mr Bartlett now occupied a small house at Highgate. The view which it commanded over the richly wooded flats of Essex, the picturesque environs of Hornsey, Hampstead, and other scenes of classic celebrity, was quite to his taste. Here,

---

* With the special exception of *Historic Notes*, by Samuel Sharpe, Esq, just published, a work of great erudition and research. To this author, the historian of ancient Egypt, our readers are indebted for the classic introduction prefixed to *The Nile Boat*, and for much interesting matter interspersed in Mr Bartlett's *Desert*, and other works. His sketch of Petra and its founders is excellent.

† See his own account, particularly his exhausting labours in obtaining facsimiles of the ancient inscriptions on the rocks, as narrated in the *Forty Days*.

among the woods and green fields, all more or less associated with the morning of life, and surrounded by his children, he found all that can sweeten labour, and shed an air of cheerful serenity on the domestic hearth. His leisure was chiefly filled up with parlour lessons to the little group, whose health, and progress in the rudiments of education, were the objects of his daily and hourly solicitude. And when these were concluded, a ramble in the adjoining wood, or on Hampstead Heath, was the usual reward of diligence and good conduct. But I must not detain the reader from a home scene which is thus vividly touched by his own pencil:

'My house is in a beautiful suburb, whence, from among a quiet covert of gardens, the last outskirts of the great city are seen meeting the open country, and its distant hum of busy life is faintly heard. My window is open, and the sunlight streams into the chamber. My youngest child[18] plays about the room. Who can paint his beauty, as, tottering to and fro with delighted activity, his round head and silken yellow curls catch the glittering rays, and the reflected light beams about his laughing countenance? What broken notes of music are the sounds of his happy voice, poured forth in the fulness of infant joy, his little cries, as a sudden gust of wind raises his curls, or some gilded insect flits, with a diamond flash, across the sunbeams? Wearied at last with play, he sinks into his little cradle, and the breathing of his rosy sleep sounds quietly through the room. Other deeply loved ones are around me – and of [those] absent, yet ever present, the images are like a familiar presence. There, touched by a master's hand, are the dear and venerable lineaments of my mother – the remains of that beauty which lingers yet in the memory of her few surviving contemporaries. But of those traces of sorrow and care, over which her serene smile sheds a melancholy grace, and which thou, painter, hast too well imitated – to me belongs the history: it is linked for ever with my own.'*

In one of those hours of mental depression – which was much aggravated at this time by professional disappointments – he writes: 'I have survived the accidents of long travel through many lands; and, though I have quitted it for ever, am within sight of the suburban home of my youth. Its green fields are beneath my eye, in the soft sunshine; its tall elms cast a tremulous shade across

---

* I have met with nothing, of a sweetly domestic character, that so nearly resembles the above as the portrait of his child in its cradle, described by a late poet. They are two cabinet pictures, on which the surviving friends of each will not hesitate to look again and again. See [Thomas] Campbell's *Letters* for 1804–5.

130

the meads, studded with daisies, and the silver light "glints" over their innumerable dew-drops. There are the old familiar paths, the hedge-rows, with their well-known gaps, and flowery borders of pansies and wild violets. Fair is the sunshine, soft and delicious the balmy breathing air, as on the first day of creation. My heart leaps up with the vivid joy of youth; and I embrace, too, with an instructed spirit, and adore with silent heart-worship, the eternal beauty that fills and blesses the universe.

'But where are those with whom I wandered in childhood about these flowery meads? Where are the friends of my riper youth, where the old familiar faces of the village? How few survivors of either! Through an opening in the trees appears the church where I received my first impressions of religion, but its very towers are changed. Where is the pastor whose sermons first awakened them? Alas! when I look back I can remember him unmarried; then, the father of a fine family, successively cut off by death! His wife departed – his spirits broken – his wretched, tottering frame! – Now he rests in peace. Of that generation scarcely a familiar face meets me save my own parents, and one or two sexagenarians, who yet linger longer. All are gone. Of my schoolfellows, how few survive, and how sad was the path of many from their thoughtless boyhood to their early graves!' Then, turning to his own position – as that of a solitary tree in the landscape – he concludes: 'But I, at least, survive; looking to my cottage hearth, in the midst of joyous existence.'

He was a strong advocate for classic study. To a young friend he gives the following advice, founded on his own personal experience:

'I cannot help pressing again and again upon you my advice, that, after acquiring so much Greek and Latin, you will not allow yourself, either by the present direction of your studies to the counting-house, or by the too natural carelessness of youth, to relax your hold upon the treasures of antiquity; but retain, at least, what you have learnt, if not rather make still further progress. I speak this to you from my own bitter experience, my dear friend, for what would I not give now to be as proficient as I once was even in Latin! And how deeply do I regret that the ill direction given to my studies excluded Greek. Never let go your classical attainments. You will deeply repent it if you do; for, be assured, they will prove the source of unspeakable pleasure and advantage hereafter.'

In the course of this year [1846] Mr Bartlett made an excursion into Wales, particularly Monmouthshire,[19] the results of which are to be seen in the new series of *Castles and Abbeys*. Among these, the illustrations of Raglan are the most remarkable; he was charmed with the subject, and never did his pencil appear to greater advantage than while delineating its picturesque remains. From Wales he proceeded into Yorkshire, where he made new sketches of Fountains and Rivaulx Abbeys, and other classic subjects, already noticed as some of his first efforts. These historical remains were revisited the following year, and from the specimens shown to me after his return, I should consider them invaluable.

In the meantime Mr Bartlett contributed various papers and illustrations which tended greatly to enhance the reputation of the magazine, of which he was editor, from March, 1849, until June, 1852. The next year [1850] he entered into an engagement with the publisher to make another trip abroad. Furnished with letters to the governor of Gibraltar, he started for the Mediterranean; and taking one of his boys with him made a pleasant and successful tour. He visited Gibraltar, Granada, Malta, and hence *The Overland Route* [1851], a work written in that pleasing and interesting style which distinguishes the whole series. The antiquarian gleanings with which the text is so happily interspersed, form a new feature, to which the archaeologist turned with satisfaction. It was recognised by the press as a 'volume full of interesting and amusing information, with an excellent historical account of Malta, many graphic sketches of travelling adventures both there and at Gibraltar, and with its engraved scenery, forming one of the most elegant volumes ever published.' 'The author conveys to us his impressions in language at once terse, concise, always graphic, and never tedious. In a word, the present work is as excellent as any of his former, remarkable for its lively and picturesque narrative, and embellished with exquisite engravings.'

The governor of Gibraltar, in letters now before me, expressed great admiration of the fidelity and effect with which the features of the old 'Rock' had been transferred to paper; and the praise of the gallant general was cordially responded to by his family. The artist could have had no higher testimony; and the success of this enterprise soon paved the way to another.

Pictures from Sicily – the result of another tour in the Mediterranean – was accomplished the following year [1852], and met with the same encouragement as its predecessors. But as the works of this series are in the hands of every reader, it is superfluous, in a limited notice like the present, to dwell on their individual and collective merits. On the subjects of which they treat, the public has assigned to them a decided pre-eminence – not only for their pictorial beauty, but for the historical, topographical, and incidental anecdotes with which they abound.

The next work of this popular series was the *Pilgrim Fathers* of New England, materials for which had been collected during his various excursions in England, Holland, and America. But, with the prospect of bringing out the work immediately, it became necessary that Mr Bartlett should cross the Atlantic for the fourth time [1852], which he happily accomplished. After spending some time among the scenes consecrated by the Pilgrim Fathers, and obtaining from their descendants in New England all the information extant, he returned to London with ample materials for the task proposed. Of the admirable taste with which the work was written and illustrated, it is superfluous to speak. It possesses, to repeat the words of a distinguished prelate, the romantic interest of *Robinson Crusoe*, with the simple and solemn dignity of the Acts of the Apostles.

Part of the following year, 1853, was spent in a second visit to Jerusalem. In the first portion of this journey he was accompanied by his brother and his eldest son whom he had the pleasure of introducing to the scenery of Interlaken and the Jungfrau.

The feelings with which Mr Bartlett revisited the scenes of his first-love, the scenes upon which he founded an honourable and lasting fame as an artist, are thus expressed in his diary at Thun: '*May*, 1853. Again in Switzerland – dear Switzerland! The well-remembered forms of the mountains rise around me like the familiar faces of old friends. The Blumlis Alp, covered with eternal snow; the pyramidal Misen, the rugged Stock-horn, the slumbering lake; the bright green stream of the Aar issuing from it, the quaint old towers of the church and castle; the blossoming orchards; the velvet meads, overhung by pine-clad heights; the rustic cottages, buried in verdure – all are beautiful as ever. But the feeling with which I now behold them is tame and poor, compared with that of twenty years ago. Like the poet, I cannot but feel sadly, "that there has passed away something from the earth," and that the freshness of early enthusiasm can never be restored.

'Yes – if the few bright hours snatched from the dull downward flow of time may be called happiness – here I was indeed happy! Youthful, and full of vigorous health, married to the wife of my choice, with life and hope before me – I possessed a gaiety and elasticity of spirits that enabled me to revel in the beauty of the surrounding scenery. This is certainly the most charming place in Switzer-

133

land. An old-fashioned house, with overhanging roofs, and trees trellised against the walls, and almost buried in fruit-trees and flowers, with steep paths behind, leading up into the wood-crowned hills, hurries my thoughts back into the past. How vivid were our enjoyments; and, I may add, how religious, how thankful was our sense of them!'

'It is not alone that twenty years and more have flown over my head, and that instead of gaily treading the upward acclivity of life, I feel that I have passed its culminating point, that the descent becomes more rapid, and the shadows fall more dark and awful as the bourne of existence is at hand! To me, no part of life has been without its appropriate enjoyments. If those proper to youth have gone, they have been replaced by others less passionate, but far more pure and deep. It is not, therefore, alone to the passage of time and feeling of decay that I must attribute the melancholy that here fills the soul – as the glacier-springs and torrents fill the hollow of an Alpine tarn, which, though stirred into a passing smile by the breeze and sunshine, speedily resumes its dark, coiled-up, self-concentrated sadness, deepened by beetling precipices, and overhung by eternal snows.'

The result of his journey to the Holy Land, was the work which appeared shortly after his death, entitled *Jerusalem Revisited*, the printing of which it became the painful duty of his brother to superintend. This, though one of the last works of his pen, was the first in his affections; for, whatever preference he might give, on certain points, to the *Desert*, his first *Walks* in and about Jerusalem, had left an impression upon his heart that no after circumstance could impair. His last visit to the Holy City had more the character of a religious pilgrimage than of a mere travelling adventure. It reminds us of the poet, Sandys, whose object in visiting Jerusalem, as his poem intimates, was to kneel at the tomb of his Saviour before descending into his own. The following Lines, addressed to Mr Bartlett on the occasion, may not inappropriately close this eventful year:

> How throbbed my heart, when through the morning skies,
> The towers of Zion met my longing eyes!
> When, one by one, along th' horizon's verge,
> I saw the hallowed landmarks first emerge;
> And felt my glorious privilege to trace
> The hills that guard Jehovah's dwelling-place!

There, gathered in majestic frame, were set
Moriah – Zion – Calvary – Olivet;
Where halos of departed glory still,
With sacred light, encompass every hill –
Where godlike forms of priests and prophets rise,
And kings, who held their sceptres from the skies,
Still cast their hallowed mantle o'er the scene,
And marshal round their 'melancholy Queen' –
The 'Queen of Nations!' Lo, how pale she stands,
With downcast look, mute lips, and claspèd hands!

On yonder height, in many a heaving mound
Of human dust, behold her battle-ground!
There, marshalled for her rescue or her fall,
Host after host has girt her sacred wall –
The Roman cohorts, and the fierce Crusade –
Moor – Moslem – Saracen – in steel arrayed;
Iberian chiefs – the Chivalry of France –
Have twang'd the bow, and hurl'd the quivering lance.

There, England's battle-axe wiped out in blood
The insults aimed at the triumphant Rood –
Rolled back the battering-rams that shook her wall –
Resolved to conquer – yet content to fall –
If here, at last, their ashes might repose
Where Jesus lived and suffered – died and rose!

Yet, widowed Queen! immortal is thy dower –
The name of God is carved on every tower!
I gaze, as if entranced! my spirit fraught
With sounds and thoughts – 'unteachable, untaught' –
Feelings, that ask for utterance in vain,
Swell in my heart, and throb within my brain.

And hark! as with slow step I muse along,
The rocks still echo to the Angels' song!
From green Gethsemané – from Siloa's wave –
From Kedron's brook – grey sepulchre and cave –

135

Each mount and vale, by saint and martyr trod,
Still shout, 'Hosannah to the Son of God!'

Thrice holy, yet unhappiest city! thou
Must wear no garland but the cypress bough!
Thy shrines are dust – thy sanctuaries defiled;
And, where thy TEMPLE stood – in triumph piled,
Omar's proud mosque usurps the hallowed place,
And drowns contempt on Israel's scattered race!

At such an hour, on such a scene to gaze,
Inspires new life, each former toil repays –
Blunts in my heart the stings of earthly care,
And crowns with rich reward the pilgrim's prayer.
For lo, at last, through scenes of various death –
Strife – storm – the desert's pestilential breath –
I touch the goal – I tread the hallowed ground
Where man was ransomed, and the Savior crowned!
Where Zion's gate, the gate of heaven appears, –
And thoughts, too deep for words, dissolve in tears!   WB

I now come to the last of many journeys, which was to terminate a career of unremitting industry, and leave a blank in that department of the fine arts in which he had no superior. He had often mentioned to me in the course of the spring, his intention of revisiting the East; but in this case, the journey was forced upon him. He looked forward to it with more aversion than pleasure, for it was not a matter of choice but of necessity. Experience had taught him what to expect in carrying out his plan, what dangers must be encountered, what expenses incurred. But, above all, the depressing circumstances under which he had accepted the commission, weighed heavily on the springs of life, and rendered his preparations for the journey irksome and compulsory. The enthusiasm with which he had entered upon former and similar enterprises had been chilled down by successive disappointments, till it subsided into feelings of apathy and indifference. He was wont to describe himself as a machine, destined to perform a certain number of revolutions, a certain *quantum* of work for its owner, then break down, and be thrown aside among the debris of implements worn out or disabled in his service.

The vexatious position in which he stood, and from which he had no means of extricating himself, told painfully upon a temperament morbidly sensitive, and produced an irritability which he struggled in vain to subdue. In him, indeed, the poetical temperament was strongly developed. The extracts from his earliest journal already quoted, demonstrate the keen sensibility of his nature. A cold look, an unkind word, was sufficient to cloud his happiness for days, and throw him back on the solitude of his own thoughts. He was thus too much at the mercy of those

'Who, without feeling, laugh at all who feel.'

Taking the sentiments of his own mind as the standard, he weighed the conduct of those with whom he had to deal by his own; and when he discovered, too late, that his conclusions were contradicted by facts, he was humbled by the conviction. Nor was his credulity on this point without its penalty; for, as in contracts, so in character, an erroneous estimate was sure to tell in the working – and in his case it was uniformly against him.

His desire to promote and ensure the health of his children, often amounted to a degree of anxiety which could only be accounted for by the extreme sensibility of his nature so often alluded to; and when any serious illness invaded the family, his entire devotion to the object, and disregard for all personal convenience and comfort, were such as I have rarely witnessed in the course of my long experience.

In all his journeys in the East, we may easily trace the current of his inmost thoughts, which pointed steadily to his own distant hearth. Incidents were often presented in these travels which greatly affected him; that, for instance, in his passage across the Desert, and again in the cloister chapel of St Catherine, on Mount Horeb. While his eye and hand were engaged on the material features of the landscape, how often did his mind revert to that moral picture – the group at his own hearth; which, in form as distinct, but as fleeting as the *mirage* itself, attended all his steps by day, and cheered the solitude of his nightly bivouac in the desert. How often was the scenery of the 'Soldier's Dream' present to his imagination – now ripening into ecstasy at his fancied return home; then fading away as the tinkling of his camel's bell dispelled the illusion and the morning light broke into his camp.

His general health at this period was apparently good; he had no organic disease, nor was he subject to any chronic ailment that interfered with his daily

137

occupations. He was active and indefatigable in the discharge of his duties; and in society his amiable manners, general information, and fund of anecdote were only surpassed by his characteristic absence of all pretension. But, though cheerful, and even buoyant in the company of private friends, the habit of his mind was that of profound thought,* which had already traced its lines deeply in the features of his countenance, radiant with intellect and benevolence, but expressive of that care and anxiety with which, by his own confession, he had been too long familiar. His happiest hours were spent in the bosom of his family, in suburban walks with his children, or in the parlour-school, in personal superintendence of lessons, and that intellectual training which is best conducted under the watchful eye of a parent.

Having a friend just returned from the seat of war to dine with me, I asked Mr Bartlett to meet him. Both familiar with the biblical and historic scenes of the East; both interested in the past, as well as in passing events; and both stored with recollections of personal adventure, their conversation was at once edifying and amusing. Having come into sudden contact with a kindred mind, he was alternately playful, serious, and descriptive; but always throwing new light upon the subject, and embodying his thoughts with so much simplicity and truth as to make a lasting impression. This was our last meeting in company; and, when I look back to it, I seem to be looking upon one of those scenes which we occasionally witness at the going down of the sun. And his own sun – though we little thought so at the time – was rapidly descending, the shadows lengthening, and the night at hand.

Passing over many little incidents by the way, I proceed at once to the morning when I took final leave of him at my own door. His parting request was, that, in case of illness in his family, I should visit and advise with them as hitherto. The request was superfluous; but it was a comfort to him at the moment to be reassured. I gave him my promise that nothing on my part should be neglected. He then moved silently towards the door – paused as if he had something more to ask, but said nothing. He seemed to part with more reluctance than on any former occasion. At last, as if by a forced effort, he again shook hands, and, with a half-audible farewell, turned hastily into the street. I never saw him again.

In this journey, as in that of the previous year, Mr Bartlett had the company

* An American poet of the highest eminence wrote, many years ago: 'Bartlett, though the most quiet, silent, and undemonstrative of men, is all that is good and amiable' [probably N.P. Willis].

of his brother as far as Strasburg where they parted, and not without a presentiment of impending evil. From Smyrna, August 7 [1854], he writes: 'When you left me, I went on by Basle to the Lake of Lucern; then over St Gothard to Milan and Venice.' 'From Trieste, I had a pleasant voyage and society to this place. The heat is excessive; but as there is a sea-breeze, I do not feel it so much as I did in Italy, where I could not sleep at all.' The immediate object of this journey was to explore the Seven Churches of Asia Minor – an enterprise for which the season was singularly unpropitious. At the moment of his arrival the country was suffering under a severe pestilence, and infested by numerous banditti, so that no step could be taken without the risk of encountering one or both. 'To robbers and pirates,' he writes, 'are now to be added cholera and quarantines, which may prevent me wholly from going to Patmos. All that I can do, is to attempt a short tour to the Seven Churches; and if I break down, I shall try to get on board the first steamer and come home.' His friends did what they could to dissuade him from exposing his life to perils at once so obvious and inevitable. But, finding that he was determined to fulfil his contract at all hazards, a trustworthy 'dragoman' was engaged to attend him; from whose notes to the consul we learn the following particulars: Mr Bartlett left Smyrna on August 5th – visited Cassaba and Sardis – and then returned after an absence of seven days. On the 13th he paid a visit for a few days to Mr James Whittal, at the village of Bournabat, about five miles from Smyrna. Here he writes, 'I meet with great kindness and hospitality. Yesterday I spent at a beautiful country house, belonging to a merchant here; so that as far as *society* goes, I get on pretty well' ... 'But this life of hazard and uncertainty is a very sad one!'

On the 18th, he set out for Ephesus, but did not visit Sochia as he had intended, on account of the cholera, which was then raging in that quarter. On the 24th, he returned to Smyrna; but, not to be detained from the personal investigation proposed, he set out for Magnesia on the 27th. From the latter he proceeded to Pergamus, and, on September 2nd, after an excursion of six days, returned without illness or accident to Smyrna. It was his fixed intention to have visited Patmos* and Samos; but learning on good authority that those waters were

---

* 'He was sadly put out,' writes a kind friend, 'in not being enabled to make his visit to Patmos. I offered him my yacht to proceed thither, and it was all agreed that he should make the voyage in her, when suddenly arrived news that the pirates had recommenced their nefarious pursuits, and the vessels from this port, on arriving at the islands, were to be subjected to quarantine on account of the cholera.'

infested by ruthless pirates, the design was reluctantly abandoned. During the whole of these journeys, as we learn from his faithful companion, Baltas, Mr Bartlett continued in good health and spirits. He made nearly fifty drawings of the most important subjects in his route. It was remarked, however, by a sympathizing friend that, 'although he had no ailments while in Smyrna, he appeared to be suffering from some pain; or rather, he betrayed the physiognomy of one "crowned with care." ' It was also observed by a lady, the wife of his friend, 'that he must have deep suffering of some nature.' But 'there was nothing of whining about him, his conversation being pleasant and animated whenever he referred to his travels in the United States and elsewhere' ... 'He was always most particular in the food he took; he travelled comfortably, taking with him an iron bedstead and tent; chose good localities to sleep upon – places distant from swampy ground. He paid his servant so much per day, to find him in horses and everything requisite for his journey. He was very much satisfied with his guide, and delivered him at parting a certificate to that effect. He always carried with him his own tea, the only beverage he made use of in his travels.' The writer then concludes:

'Mr Bartlett was introduced to me by our clergyman on his arrival; and, as he lived in a hotel next door to my house, we became very intimate. It has pained me beyond measure to hear of his death. He was so gentle, so gentlemanly, that he really fascinated us all. He seemed to be a most devoted father. In an il-lustrated London paper at my house there was a sketch of a miniature regatta in one of the Hampstead ponds. When he saw it his heart seemed to dilate in thinking of home! The scenery, he told me, was most familiar to him, as he was in the frequent habit of walking along the banks of the pond with his children, of whom he often spoke.'

Finding that all further progress in the investigation of his subject was impracticable, his halt at Smyrna was very short. Hearing, on the very morning of his return from Magnesia, that the French mail steamer was to depart in a few hours, he engaged a passage in her; and, bidding a hasty farewell to the consul, and other kind friends, he immediately embarked in the 'Egypt.' From that hour until the scene closed upon him for ever, the story of the voyage is soon told.

When they anchored at Malta he went ashore for a few hours, renewed his acquaintance with some of the principal objects of that remarkable island, partook of some light repast, and then returned on board. Owing to his previously exhausted state of health, the effort to see much in a few hours had been too great. But thinking that some additional refreshment would relieve the sense of fatigue under which he laboured, he sat down to table with his fellow passengers, partook of the evening meal, and entered into conversation with apparent cheerfulness. He then retired; and with symptoms of increasing debility, soon betook himself to his berth – but it was not to find the relief he sought. Becoming more and more restless as the morning advanced, the medical officer was called to his side, and found him much excited – and expressing his conviction that the hand of death was upon him.

The surgeon did what he could to relieve the urgent symptoms; and for a little while the means employed appeared to take effect. But the hopes thus awakened were soon baffled, and finally extinguished by the symptoms of absolute prostration under which he was gradually, but visibly sinking. He never rallied: and, at length, calmly expired at eight o'clock in the evening of September 13 [1854]. His death[20] took place in the presence of Colonel Onslow, of the Fusilier Guards; Mr Purdie, Queen's Messenger; and the surgeon of the vessel; who, after taking a note of the personal effects of the deceased, made preparations for the last solemn scene.

Early next morning, the British passengers and the officers of the ship formed themselves into a little circle at the side of the vessel. The aide-de-camp of Lord De Ros, then on board, read the impressive service for burial at sea. This being concluded, the remains of our lamented friend, enclosed in a hasty shroud, were slowly raised by the hands of strangers – then lowered at a given signal, and consigned to their ocean grave.

> The prayer is said,
> And the last rite man pays to man is paid;
> The plashing water marks his resting-place,
> And folds him round in one long cold embrace;
> Bright bubbles for a moment sparkle o'er,
> Then break to be, like him, beheld no more!

To the talents of a most accomplished artist – an able, pleasing, and instructive writer – and of a traveller, whose pen and pencil sketches are universally admired, Mr Bartlett united those higher qualities of mind and heart which singularly endeared him to his friends. To a peculiarly high sense of honour was united a most generous and affectionate nature – content to bear any personal sacrifice

141

for the sake of others. Thus a mutual bond of attachment was formed which was strengthened and confirmed by years. That bond was suddenly torn asunder. He was summoned hence at short notice, in the prime of life, in the maturity of his genius, at an hour when every friendly hand was extended to welcome his return – an event to which we had blindly looked forward as the long-expected dawn of his better fortunes.

He has left it in writing that, during a period of twenty years – down to the hour of his death – the fruit of his incessant labour was barely sufficient to maintain his wife and children in credit and respectability; and that, with all his earnest endeavours to accomplish so desirable an end, he could never secure any permanent share or copyright in the numerous works by which his name has been rendered so popular at home and abroad. In the eminent position to which he raised himself, as an artist and author, he was never cheered with anything beyond the vague hope of independence. But in his works he has left the public a noble monument of his genius; and to his family he has bequeathed the still more precious inheritance of a spotless reputation.

> Alas! on his untimely bier,
>   Deep, deep beneath the billow;
> We cannot drop the kindred tear,
>   Nor, weeping, plant the willow!
>
> No grave has he in church-yard mound,
>   Where Hope her watch is keeping;
> But Ocean's bed is 'hallow'd ground' –
>   For there his dust is sleeping!
>
> No 'stone' records the brief 'Here lies' –
>   To worth and genius given;
> But, strong in faith, we raise our eyes,
>   And read his name in Heaven![21]

Appendix

The following translation (in Mr Bartlett's handwriting) of an original letter was found among his papers from abroad. It shows the state of the country around Smyrna on his arrival in August, and is thus endorsed by him: 'Brought by a peasant, who seemed terrified out of his life. Mr W gave it to the Pasha, who turned very pale, and said – "leave the answer to me"; and two or three days afterwards a man came to say that "the heads of the men were at Mr W's disposal." '

'To the respectable Mr W –
Sir,
   We took the liberty of sending you on the 16th of this month a letter, with the intention of placing you among the number of our benefactors. But, while we were anxiously awaiting the fruits of your benevolence, we saw, with the greatest astonishment, the shepherd sent to you coming towards us, followed by a troop of guards. Not being certain by whom these fellows ... we have come to the decision of writing you a second time, because it seemed strange to us that a gentlemen like you could stoop to become an informer. We did not ask you for thirty, or fifty, or a hundred thousand piastres, that you should have felt so much displeased. We only asked you for a trifling sum, (£100) just to meet our expenses for the few next days. If we wished to do you a mischief, we knew very well when to find the occasion; but vagabonds as we may be considered to be, we have hitherto respected you, and shall still observe the regard due to your character. But know, nevertheless, that, if a man determines to revenge a thing, he is carried away like the most savage animal. We beg of you, then, to send us a reply, in order to set us at our ease. Men ought not be imprisoned without the slightest motive. We are robbers – and

143

if we fell in with the sultan himself, we would give him our letter to carry to its address; and if he refused, we would make him change his religion seven times over. We tell you that we fear neither the Pasha nor any one else, God alone excepted; and it depends on you to do what you may consider prudent.

Awaiting your reply, we remain yours,

STELLIO & CO.'

Copy of agreement with his Dragoman at Smyrna, August, 1854.

'M. Bartlett convient avec M. Baltass de lui payer £1 10s. par jour en route; et pour les jours de repos £1 par jour. M. Baltass est obligé de fournir tout le necessaire pour le voyage, tant chevaux, nourriture, etc, d'une manière comfortable. M. Bartlett, s'il se trouve indisposé, peut revenir tout-suite en payant les jours de son absence.

M. Bartlett a payé sur sa compte dix livres turcs.

(Signé)   W.H. BARTLETT.
EMANUEL BALTASS,
Dragoman.'

BRIEF EXTRACTS FROM LETTERS

The India Board, February 3, 1845 I visited the Holy City this autumn with Mr Bartlett's *Walks about Jersualem* in my hand; and I do not hesitate to say it is by far the most satisfactory Guide that I have seen.   J. EMERSON TENNENT

Chesham Place, May 24 Of the *Sketches of Jerusalem*, their boldness and fidelity are marvellous; and I was highly delighted with the exactness of the delineations of the various localities.
                                                     CASTLEREAGH

April 8, 1848 We return your beautiful and very interesting book, *Forty Days in the Desert*. Many thanks for the pleasure we have received from it. It does the Author *the highest credit as an artist and a writer* ... Yesterday Dr Lushington called, and after examining it, took down the publisher's name, that he might get a copy for himself. It is, indeed, a very attractive work, and my sister has enjoyed it ...   JOANNA BAILLIE

Sunny Side, Dec. 21, 1852 To the number of Bartlett's *History of the United States*, I have been able to give but a cursory inspection. That, however, has been sufficient to satisfy me of the merit of the work. It appears to be written in a spirit of truth and candour. *Facts are clearly and fairly stated in a pure, perspicuous style, generally concise and often highly graphic.* It is a work that wins the confidence of the reader. Of the engravings with which it is illustrated and embellished I cannot speak too highly – they are admirable. WASHINGTON IRVING

From the late Governor of Gibraltar, Jan. 9, 1851 Your beautiful volumes on 'Malta' and this noble 'Rock,' I shall often, I assure you, look over with the highest gratification. I am very partial to this place from its magnificent bay, and views from the rock, which delight me continually. But, apart from these, you have in the text touched upon a subject which is of the greatest interest to me, involving, as it does, the commercial welfare of the Gibraltar community. I should have said *destroying*, instead of involving – I mean the smuggling – which is the bane of moral, commercial, and every other welfare here.

From other members of the Governor's family. Gibraltar, Jan. 15, 1851 The engravings of Gibraltar are by far the best we have ever seen. They have been universally admired here as being so particularly correct, and, apart from their merit as works of art, giving so good an idea of the place.

I fully concur in the above. I shall immediately prepare a copy for our library, *as it is quite a standard work on our Mediterranean fortresses.*

Oct. 29, 1853 ... I have thought much of the end and result of all your great labours and the time spent, and wish that you and I had come together fifteen years ago, it would have been better for us both. T

May 13, 1854 I feel myself under great obligation to you – so extreme is the pleasure I have in your illustration of the countries I have travelled through. Here is your *Holy Land* on my shelves; and *Switzerland*, the *Danube*, and the *United States*, are the prettiest books in my library, and more than that to me. HARRIET MARTINEAU

145

List of Mr W.H.Bartlett's Works

Works illustrated by Mr W.H. Bartlett

1 ESSEX – HISTORY AND TOPOGRAPHY OF THE COUNTY OF. By Wm Wright, MA, FAS. Embellished with 101 Engravings, from Drawings by W.H. Bartlett, Esq, and others. Two vols. 4to

2 SWITZERLAND. By Wm Beattie, MD. Illustrated by W.H. Bartlett, Esq. Two vols. 4to. 1836

3 SCOTLAND. By Wm Beattie, MD. Illustrated by T. Allom, Esq, W.H. Bartlett, Esq, etc. Two vols. 4to

4 THE PORTS, HARBOURS, COAST SCENERY, AND WATERING PLACES OF GREAT BRITAIN. Vol. II. By Wm Beattie, MD. Illustrated by W.H. Bartlett, J.D. Harding, Creswick, and other Artists. Two vols. 4to

5 SYRIA AND THE HOLY LAND, ASIA MINOR, etc. Illustrated by W.H. Bartlett, Wm Purser, etc. 4to. 1837

6 HOLLAND AND BELGIUM. By Professor Van Kampen, of Amsterdam. Illustrated by W.H. Bartlett, Esq. One vol., royal 8vo

7 THE WALDENSES; OR, PROTESTANT VALLEYS OF PIEDMONT AND DAUPHINY. By Wm Beattie, MD. Illustrated by Messrs Bartlett and Brockedon. One vol. 4to. 1837

8 THE BEAUTIES OF THE BOSPHORUS. By Miss Pardoe. Illustrated by W.H. Bartlett. One vol. 4to. 1840

9 AMERICAN SCENERY. By N.P. Willis, Esq. Illustrated by W.H. Bartlett. Two vols. 4to

10 CANADIAN SCENERY. By N.P. Willis, Esq. Illustrated by W.H. Bartlett. Two vols. 4to. 1842

11 THE DANUBE. By Wm Beattie, MD. Illustrated by W.H. Bartlett. One vol. 4to

12 IRELAND – THE SCENERY AND ANTIQUITIES OF. Illustrated by W.H. Bartlett. The literary portion by N.P. Willis and J. Stirling Coyne, Esqrs. Two vols. 4to

13 THE CHRISTIAN IN PALESTINE; OR, Scenes of Sacred History. Illustrated by W.H. Bartlett. With Explanatory Descriptions by the Rev. Henry Stebbing, DD

14 THE LIFE AND EPISTLES OF ST PAUL. By the Rev. W.J. Conybeare, MA, and the

Rev. J.S. Howson, MA. Illustrated by W.H. Bartlett. Two vols. 4to. 1852

15 THE PICTORIAL HISTORY OF SCOTLAND, with Illustrations on Steel from Drawings by W.H. Bartlett, and other Artists[22]

16 THE CASTLES AND ABBEYS OF ENGLAND. By Wm Beattie, MD. New Series. Illustrated by W.H. Bartlett, Esq, and other Artists

Works written and illustrated by Mr W.H. Bartlett

17 WALKS ABOUT THE CITY AND ENVIRONS OF JERUSALEM. 8vo. 1844

18 VIEWS ILLUSTRATING THE TOPOGRAPHY OF JERUSALEM, Ancient and Modern. 1845. Folio[23]

19 FORTY DAYS IN THE DESERT, on the Track of the Israelites; or, a Journey from Cairo, by Wady Feiran to Mount Sinai and Petra. 1848. Sup. roy. 8vo

20 THE NILE BOAT, or Glimpses of the Land of Egypt. 1849. Sup. roy. 8vo

21 GLEANINGS, PICTORIAL AND ANTIQUARIAN ON THE OVERLAND ROUTE. Sup. roy. 8vo

22 FOOTSTEPS OF OUR LORD, and His Apostles, in Syria, Greece, and Italy. 1851. Sup. roy. 8vo

23 PICTURES FROM SICILY. 1852. Sup. roy. 8vo

24 THE PILGRIM FATHERS; or, the Founders of New England in the Reign of James the First. Sup. roy. 8vo

25 JERUSALEM REVISITED. 1854. Sup. roy. 8vo

26 SCRIPTURE SITES AND SCENES, from Actual Survey, in Egypt, Arabia, and Palestine. Illustrated. Post 8vo[24]

27 THE HISTORY OF AMERICA. By W.H. Bartlett. Continued by Mr B.B. Woodward. Illustrated. 4to

28 THE WILKIE GALLERY; with Notices Biographical and Critical. Eliphant 4to

MEM. – The *Walks* and *Forty Days* had each, before the author's death, reached at least a fourth edition; the *Nile Boat*, and the *Footsteps*, a third edition; and the *Overland Route*, and the *Pilgrim Fathers*, a second edition.

Mr B was editor of *Sharpe's London Magazine* from March, 1849 to June, 1852, during which time, and previously thereto, he made various contributions to it.[25]

In 1851, a Panorama of Jerusalem and the Holy Land was painted from Mr B's drawings; and is, I believe, still exhibiting in Ireland.

Mr B paid six visits to the East, viz, in 1834–5 – 1837 – 1842 – 1845 – 1853 – 1854; and four visits to America, viz, in 1836–7 – 1838 – 1841, and 1852.

The above list does not include the works brought out by Mr John Britton, which are prior to any in the list, and to which Mr Bartlett contributed drawings: among which works are,
Cathedral Antiquities
Picturesque Antiquities of English Cities

Mary S. Rickerby, Printer, 73 Cannon Street, City

Notes to Memoir

1 John Britton, *Cathedral Antiquities. Historical and Descriptive Accounts* ... 5 vols. London, Nattali, 1836

2 John Britton, *Picturesque Antiquities of the English Cities, Illustrated by a Series of Engravings of Ancient Buildings* ... London, Nattali, 1836

3 Perhaps Mary Wollstonecraft Shelley, who bought the Bartlett home at 5 Bartholomew Place in 1824.

4 Thomas Wright, *The History and Topography of Essex Comprising its Ancient and Modern History* ... 2 vols. London, George Virtue, I, 1831; II 1835

5 Comte D'Orsay had settled in London in 1831, where he soon became well known in artistic and fashionable circles.

6 Carne, *Syria, the Holy Land, Asia Minor*

7 See references to F. Catherwood in W.H. Bartlett's *Walks about Jerusalem* and *Jerusalem Revisited*. For Catherwood's life, see Victor von Hagen, *Catherwood, Architect – Explorer of Two Worlds* (Pennsylvania, Barre, 1968). Joseph Bonomi (1796–1878), sculptor and draftsman, travelled in Egypt, 1824–32;

in 1833 he accompanied Catherwood on his journey to the Sinai and to the Holy Land. See *Dictionary of National Biography*.

8 Dr W.S. Gilly (1789–1855)

9 South of Briançon in Dauphine, France

10 Alphonse de Lamartine, *Souvenirs, impressions, pensèes et paysages, pendant un voyage en Orient, 1832–33* ... Paris 1835

11 See Thomas Campbell, *Gertrude of Wyoming; a Pennsylvanian Tale*. London, Longman, Hurst, Rees, and Orme, 1809

12 A banking firm in the Strand

13 The Countess of Blessington who, from 1833 on, was one of Dr William Beattie's close friends.

14 William Beattie, *The Ports, Harbours, Watering-Places and Coast Scenery of Great Britain* ... 2 vols. London, George Virtue, 1842

15 N.P. Willis and J. Stirling Coyne, *The Scenery and Antiquities of Ireland*. 2 vols. London, George Virtue, 1842

16 *Sharpe's London Magazine*, XIV, 95–7. This was the third tour if we assume, as I think we must, that Bartlett went to Ireland to do the sketches for *Ireland Illustrated*, 1831.

17 Samuel Carter Hall, *Ireland: its Scenery, Character, etc.* 3 vols. London, How and Parsons, 1841–3

18 Thomas Lemon

19 Monmouthshire is in England. Bartlett engravings of six Welsh scenes appear in *The Tourist in Wales* ... London, George Virtue, [1851]

20 Bartlett probably died of cholera, which was very prevalent in the Mediterranean and Middle East throughout 1854. George Evelyn Palmer's *A Diary of the Crimea* (London, Duckworth, 1954) notes that the *Egyptus* in late July 1854 had numerous cases of cholera among its passengers and that on its passage from Marseilles fifteen deaths occurred on board and fourteen men were put ashore in Malta in a dying state.

21 Lines written by William Beattie

22 Published [1852]–1859

23 This is the only Bartlett work I have been unable to locate.

24 Published [1849]

25 According to the prefaces attached to *Sharpe's London Magazine* (January–June 1852; and July–December 1852), Bartlett relinquished his position as editor in January 1852, when the management was placed 'under the conduct of Mrs S.C. Hall.'

Bibliography

BOOKS WRITTEN BY OR CONTAINING
ILLUSTRATIONS BY W.H. BARTLETT DURING
THE YEARS, 1826–56

Bartlett, William Henry. *Footsteps of Our Lord and his Apostles in Syria, Greece, and Italy*. London, Arthur Hall, Virtue, 1851
– *Forty Days in the Desert, on the Track of the Israelites*. 5th ed. London, Arthur Hall, nd. First published in 1848
– *Gleanings, Pictorial and Antiquarian, on the Overland Route*. London, Hall, Virtue, 1851
– *The History of the United States of North America* ... Continued by B.B. Woodward. 3 vols. New York, George Virtue, [1856]
– *Jerusalem Revisited*. London, Arthur Hall, Virtue, 1855
– *The Nile Boat; or, Glimpses of the Land of Egypt*. London, Arthur Hall, Virtue, 1849
– *Original Drawings*. Folio held in the library of the University of Guelph
– *Pictures from Sicily*. London, Arthur Hall, Virtue, 1853
– *The Pilgrim Fathers; or, The Founders of New England in the Reign of James the First*. London, Arthur Hall, Virtue, 1853
– *Scripture Sites and Scenes*. London, Arthur Hall, [1849]
– *Views Illustrating the Topography of Jerusalem, Ancient and Modern*. 1845. Folio
– *Walks About the City and Environs of Jerusalem*. London, George Virtue, 1844
– *The Wilkie Gallery with Biographical and Critical Notices*. London & New York, George Virtue, nd
Beattie, William. *The Castles and Abbeys of England*. 2 vols. London, Virtue, [1844]
– *The Danube: Its History, Scenery, and Topography*. London, Virtue, 1844
– *The Ports, Harbours, Watering-Places, and Coast Scenery of Great Britain*. 2 vols. London, George Virtue, 1842. First published under the title *Finden's Views of the Ports, Harbours and Watering Places of Great Britain. Continued by W.H. Bartlett*. London, George Virtue, 1839
– *Scotland Illustrated*. 2 vols. London, George Virtue, 1838. A later edition, no date, containing eleven Bartlett prints in

an appendix to vol. II, bears the title, *Caledonia Illustrated*.

– *Switzerland Illustrated*. 2 vols. London, Virtue, 1836

– *The Waldenses, or Protestant Valleys of Piedmont, Dauphiny, and the Ban de la Roche*. London, George Virtue, 1838

Britton, John. *Cathedral Antiquities: Historical and Descriptive Accounts ...* 5 vols. London, M.A. Nattali, 1821–36

– *Chronological History and Graphic Illustrations of Christian Architecture in England*. London, M.A. Nattali, 1826. Vol. 5 of *The Architectural Antiquities of Great Britain*

– *Picturesque Antiquities of the English Cities*. London, M.A. Nattali, 1836. First published: London, Longman, Rees, Orme, Brown, and Green; the Author and J. Le Keux, 1830

Britton John, and E.W. Brayley. *Devonshire and Cornwall Illustrated*. London, H. Fisher, R. Fisher, and P. Jackson, 1832

Carne, John. *Syria, the Holy Land, Asia Minor etc.* 3 vols. London, Fisher, Son, 1836–[1838]

Conybeare, W.J., and J.S. Howson. *The Life and Epistles of St. Paul*. 2 vols. London, Longman, Brown, Green, and Longmans, 1853

Cunningham, Allan, ed. *The Poems, Letters, and Land of Robert Burns*. 2 vols. London, George Virtue, [1840]

Kampen, N.G. van. *The History and Topography of Holland and Belgium*. London, George Virtue, [1837]

Pardoe, Julia. *The Beauties of the Bosphorus*. London, Virtue, 1839

Stebbing, Henry. *The Christian in Palestine, or Scenes of Sacred History*. London, George Virtue, [1847]

Taylor, James. *The Pictorial History of Scotland*. 2 vols. London, Virtue, [1852]–1859

The Tourist in Wales: A Series of Views of Picturesque Scenery, Towns, Castles, Antiquities, etc. London, George Virtue, [1851]

The Watering Places of Great Britain and Fashionable Directory Illustrated with Views. London, I.T. Hinton, 1831

Willis, N.P. *American Scenery; or Land, Lake, and River*. 2 vols. London, George Virtue, 1840

– *Canadian Scenery Illustrated*. 2 vols. London, George Virtue, 1842

– *The Scenery and Antiquities of Ireland*. 2 vols. London, George Virtue, [1842]

Wright, George N. *Ireland Illustrated*. London, H. Fisher, Son, and Jackson, 1831

– *The Rhine, Italy, and Greece*. 2 vols. London, Fisher, Son, 1841

– *The Shores and Islands of the Mediterranean*. London, Fisher, Son, [1840]

Wright, Thomas. *The History and Topography of the County of Essex Comprising its Ancient and Modern History*. 2 vols. London, George Virtue, 1831–5

GENERAL BIBLIOGRAPHY

Barbier, Carl Paul. *William Gilpin*. Oxford, Clarendon, 1963

[Barteaux, Eleanor]. 'Bibliography, William Henry Bartlett, 1809–1854,' *Ontario Library Review*, May 1945

Barteaux, Eleanor. 'W.H. Bartlett, of "Bartlett Prints",' *Dalhousie Review*, January 1945

Bartlett, William Henry. *Bartlett's Canada, a pre-Confederation Journey*. Introduction by Henry C. Campbell. Texts by Janice

Tyrwhitt. Toronto, McClelland and Stewart, 1968

– *Quebec 1800: a Nineteenth Century Romantic Sketch of Quebec. Un essai de gravures romantiques sur le pays de Québec au XIX siècle.* Text by Michel Brunet and J. Russell Harper. [Montreal], Les Editions de l'Homme, 1968

Beers, Henry A. *Nathaniel Parker Willis.* Boston, Houghton Mifflin, 1893

Britton, John. 'Mr William Henry Bartlett' (an obituary notice), *The Art-Journal,* 1 Jan. 1855

– *The Auto-Biography.* London, The Author, 1850

– *The History and Antiquities of the Cathedral Church of Worcester.* London, Nattali, 1836

– *The History and Antiquities of the Metropolitan Church of Canterbury.* London, Nattali, 1836

Burke, Edmund. *A Philosophical Enquiry into the Origin of our Ideas of the Sublime and Beautiful.* Ed. by J.T. Boulton. London, Routledge and Kegan Paul, 1958

Clark, Kenneth. *Landscape into Art.* Boston, Beacon Press, 1961

Clifford, Derek. *Watercolours of The Norwich School.* London, Cory, Adams and Mackay, 1965

Collard, Elizabeth. *Nineteenth Century Pottery and Porcelain in Canada.* Montreal, McGill University Press, 1967

Cowdrey, Bartlett. 'William Henry Bartlett and the American Scene,' *Proceedings of the New York State Historical Association.* New York, xxxix, 1941

Earl, Mary-Ellen. *William H. Bartlett and his Imitators.* New York, W.F. Humphrey, 1966

Ferriday, Peter. 'A Victorian Journeyman Artist,' *Country Life,* 15 Feb. 1968

Gilpin, William. *An Essay upon Prints: containing Remarks upon the Principles of Picturesque Beauty; the Different Kinds of Prints; and the Characters of the Most Noted Masters ...* 2nd ed. London, G. Scott, 1768

– *Observations Relative Chiefly to Picturesque Beauty, Made in the Year 1776, on Several Parts of Great Britain; particularly the Highlands of Scotland.* 2 vols. London, R. Blamire, 1789

Godenrath, Percy F. *Catalogue of the Manoir Richelieu Collection of Canadiana.* Montreal, 1930, 1939

Hennepin, Father Louis. *A New Discovery of a Vast Country in America.* Reprinted from the second London issue of 1698 by Reuben Gold Thwaites. 2 vols. Chicago, A.C. McLurg, 1903

Heriot, George. *Travels Through the Canadas, Containing a Description of the Picturesque Scenery on Some of the Rivers and Lakes ...* London, Richard Phillips, 1807

Hipple, Walter John, Jr. *The Beautiful, the Sublime and the Picturesque in Eighteenth Century British Aesthetic Theory.* Carbondale, Southern Illinois University Press, 1957

Hughes, C.E. *Early English Water-Colour.* Rev. and ed. by Jonathan Mayne. London, Benn, 1950

Hussey, Christopher. *The Picturesque, Studies in a Point of View.* London, Frank Cass, 1967

Lamartine, De Prat, Marie Louis Alphonse de. *Voyage en Orient.* Ed. Lotfy Fam. Paris, Librairie Nizet, nd

Lear, Edward. *Journals of a Landscape Painter in Southern Calabria etc.* London, Richard Bentley, 1852.

Malins, Edward. *English Landscaping and*

Literature, 1660–1840. London, Oxford, 1966

Manwaring, Elizabeth. *Italian Landscape in Eighteenth-Century England*. London, Cass, 1925

Morisset, Gérard. 'La peinture traditionnelle au Canada français,' *l'Encyclopédie du Canada français*. Vol. II. Ottawa, Le Cercle du Livre de France, 1960

– *Peintures et tableaux, les arts au Canada français*. Quebec, les Editions du Chevalet, 1936

Morse, Eric W. 'Canoe Routes of the Voyageurs: the Geography and Logistics of the Canadian Fur Trade,' *Canadian Geographical Journal*, LXIII, July 1961

Muddiman, Bernard, 'The Bartlett Drawings,' *Canadian Magazine*, Jan. 1914

Roscoe, Thomas. *The Tourist in Spain, Biscay, and the Castiles*. Illus. by David Roberts. London, Robert Jennings, 1837

Ruskin, John. *Modern Painters*. 2nd ed.,

vol. IV. London, George Allan, 1900

Sadleir, Michael. *Blessington-D'Orsay, a Masquerade*. London, Constable, 1933

Searight, Sara. *The British in the Middle East*. London, Weidenfeld and Nicolson, 1969

Spendlove, F. St. George. *The Face of Early Canada*. Toronto, Ryerson [1958]

Templeman, William D. *The Life and Work of William Gilpin*. Urbana, University of Illinois Press, 1939

[Traill, Catherine Parr]. *The Backwoods of Canada: Being the Letters from the Wife of an Emigrant Officer* ... London, Charles Knight, 1836

Willis, Nathaniel Parker. *Canadian Scenery Illustrated*. Facsimile edition. 2 vols. Toronto, Peter Martin Associates, 1967

– *Rural Letters and Other Records of Thought at Leisure*. Auburn, Alden, Beardsley, 1854

Index

Illustration Credits

This book
was designed by
ALLAN FLEMING

the plates
were prepared and
printed by
HERZIG-SOMERVILLE LIMITED

the typographic composition
and
printing of the text
was by
UNIVERSITY OF
TORONTO
PRESS